Controls and Choices

Controls and Choices

The Educational Marketplace and the Failure of School Desegregation

Carl L. Bankston III and Stephen J. Caldas

ROWMAN & LITTLEFIELD
Lanham • Boulder • New York • London

Published by Rowman & Littlefield
A wholly owned subsidiary of The Rowman & Littlefield Publishing Group, Inc.
4501 Forbes Boulevard, Suite 200, Lanham, Maryland 20706
www.rowman.com

Unit A, Whitacre Mews, 26-34 Stannary Street, London SE11 4AB

British Library Cataloguing in Publication Information Available

Library of Congress Cataloging-in-Publication Data

Bankston, Carl L. (Carl Leon), 1952-
Controls and choices : the educational marketplace and the failure of school desegregation / Carl L. Bankston, III and Stephen J. Caldas.
p. cm.
Includes bibliographical references and index.
ISBN 978-1-4758-1468-2 (cloth : alk. paper) -- ISBN 978-1-4758-1469-9 (pbk. : alk. paper) -- ISBN 978-1-4758-1470-5 (electronic)
1. Segregation in education--Economic aspects--United States. 2. School integration--Economic aspects--United States. 3. Educational change--Economic aspects--United States. 4. School districts--Management--United States. 5. Educational vouchers--United States. 6. Charter schools--United States. I. Caldas, Stephen J., 1957- II. Title.
LC212.52.B36 2015
379.2'630973--dc23

2015017712

∞ ™ The paper used in this publication meets the minimum requirements of American National Standard for Information Sciences Permanence of Paper for Printed Library Materials, ANSI/NISO Z39.48-1992.

Printed in the United States of America

To Cynthia and Suzanne, public school teachers

Contents

Introduction

When we first began working together on studies of school desegregation in the 1990s, we were consistently struck by the fact that it never seemed to have worked. In our first book on efforts to desegregate schools, *A Troubled Dream: The Promise and Failure of School Desegregation in Louisiana,* [1] we looked in detail at the history of this effort to bring greater equality to education in a state that had a long record of racial oppression and discrimination. It would have been comforting to find that the schools in Louisiana had made progress after early conflicts over integration.

In fact, though, we found that de facto segregation not only continued, but often intensified following court-mandated desegregation. Moreover, although we acknowledged that racial prejudice and racially discriminatory practices still existed, we found that racism could not account for contemporary separate and unequal education. Instead, we found that most de facto segregation was driven by socially and economically advantaged families, disproportionately white, avoiding and fleeing from schools attended by socially and economically disadvantaged students, mostly minority.

We extended our investigation to schools throughout the nation, and set out our findings in *Forced to Fail: The Paradox of School Desegregation.* [2] There, we saw many of the same dynamics that we had seen operating in Louisiana in play nationwide. The present book and a companion volume, *Still Failing: The Continuing Paradox of School Desegregation*, bring the findings of *Forced to Fail* into the second decade of the twenty-first century, and offer more detailed empirical and theoretical explanations of these findings.

This book concentrates on how schools form an educational marketplace and why desegregation has failed because it involved monopolistic efforts at redistributing opportunities. These efforts were fundamentally at odds with the self-interest of those who had the greatest ability to make choices in the educational marketplace. The companion volume focuses on the related issue of how social capital has shaped those self-interests throughout the history of American school desegregation.

BACKGROUND: THE EVOLUTION OF EDUCATIONAL REDISTRIBUTION

In order to understand why many Americans have been deeply committed to campaigns to redistribute students by race in our public schools, we need to begin by recognizing that these commitments do not simply arise out of utopian theories aimed at constructing an egalitarian future. Instead, school desegregation programs evolved from a series of reactions to a historical heritage of racial and ethnic discrimination that contradicted basic American political ideals.

During the centuries from the beginnings of European and African settlement in North America through the end of legal race-based slavery after the U.S. Civil War, Americans of African ancestry had virtually no access to formal education. It was, in fact, against the law in many slave-holding states to teach slaves to read. During the late nineteenth and early twentieth centuries, when the modern system of public education developed in the United States, public education did become widely available to African Americans. However, this education was limited, separate, and highly unequal.[3]

In the early twentieth century, African Americans and whites concerned with racial justice began to organize political responses to continuing racial legal, social, and economic disadvantages. One of the most important of these responses was the National Association for the Advancement of Colored People (NAACP), established in 1910. In the late 1940s, the Legal Defense and Education Fund of the NAACP began a struggle to end the segregation of American educational institutions.

The NAACP, acting through its Legal Defense Fund (as it is usually called) initiated a series of lawsuits that argued that segregated schooling had led to gross inequalities between the schools attended by white children and those attended by black children. These suits culminated in the famous *Brown v. Board of Education of Topeka* decisions, in which the Supreme Court declared that racial discrimination in education was unconstitutional and called for admission to public schools on a racially nondiscriminatory basis.[4] Along with advocating judicial action, the growing Civil Rights Movement pushed for greater racial equality in all areas of American life.

Responding to the Civil Rights Movement, the federal government began expanding its power to intervene in situations of racial discrimination. The Civil Rights Act of 1957 created the Civil Rights Division of the Department of Justice, and it gave the U.S. Attorney General the power to sue on behalf of black citizens who had suffered discrimination in federal elections. This power to sue was expanded as the Civil Rights Division was charged with enforcing provisions of the Civil Rights Acts of 1960, 1964, and 1968, and the Voting Rights Act of 1965.[5]

The development of the Civil Rights Division meant that the federal government came to play a dual role in desegregation lawsuits. It provided both the judiciary and attorneys for parties who charged that a given school system was illegally segregated, by an expanding definition of segregation also created by the federal government. Government direction of resources is the key to a redistributive economy. Under the mechanisms developing in the late 1950s and early 1960s, the Department of Justice could charge that educational resources were unjustly allocated and the federal judiciary could order some kind of reallocation.

In the companion volume to this book, we divide the history of desegregation into six distinct periods. The first period, which we date from the Supreme Court's two *Brown* decisions of 1954 and 1955 to the Civil Rights Act of 1964, involved simply trying to get school districts to accept the Court's mandate that students be allowed to enroll in public schools regardless of race. The second period, in the mid-1960s immediately following the Civil Rights Act, was the "freedom of choice" period. Schools could not bar black or other minority students,[6] but they also did not have to make any special efforts to enroll them.

The main problem with "freedom of choice" was that given the "choice," white and minority students often remained in separate schools. If inequality in education was a product of the fact of segregation and not a problem of its legal requirement, then allowing free choice did little to address inequality. Moreover, students of different races often attended different schools because of the past or even present decisions of school boards in matters such as drawing attendance boundaries. Local school districts had arguably established deeply ingrained inequalities through their intentional policies and actions.

Because "freedom of choice" did not end educational inequality by race and ethnicity, the Department of Justice and the federal judiciary pushed further, with the support of some concerned citizens and against the protests of others. The Supreme Court's 1968 decision in the *Green v. New Kent County School Board* case[7] began a third period of maximum governmental involvement in trying to redistribute students by race among schools, through busing, closing schools to merge student populations, and by other court-directed strategies.

The third, post-*Green* period, was a time of conflict over public schools. As we detail in our case histories of districts in chapters 3 and 4, the late 1960s and 1970s saw anger, protests, and riots over the desegregation of schools. This was also the time when school districts began to see "white flight" from desegregating locations, often in urban locations with large minority populations. *Green* also, though, contained the seeds of future periods in educational policy. Recognizing that districts were required to redistribute students to make up for inequalities the districts themselves had created, *Green* enunciated the concept of "unitary status," in which a district had done everything possible to eliminate vestiges of past discrimination.

Other court decisions also began to lay the groundwork for less aggressive educational redistribution. Notably, the Supreme Court greatly limited, and in most cases outlawed, reaching across district boundaries to ship students between mainly white residential areas and mainly minority residential areas. A fifth period, marked by the judiciary's willingness to release "compliant" school districts from the scrutiny of federal oversight, began in earnest during the 1980s. Significant numbers of districts were granted unitary status, and control of school districts was in many cases returned to popularly elected school boards.

We identify our current era, in the first decades of the twenty-first century, as beginning a sixth period. Although some districts remain under desegregation orders, we can see a definite tendency to back away from efforts to redistribute students across schools by race. Among the successors to racial desegregation policies, the "school choice" reforms that we discuss in chapter 5 are among the most prominent. These last two periods, though, raise the questions of why desegregation did not create a truly racially integrated and egalitarian school system and why courts and policy makers began to back away from attempts to redistribute students.

We argue that there are basically two competing answers to these questions. The first is the "failure of will" answer. According to this view, forced transfers of students and other aggressive judicially mandated policies would lead to greater equality in education if only legislators and judges had the will to continue trying to make school districts conform to plans for redesigning schools and even American society. Our fifth and sixth periods, from this point of view, essentially involve retreat from the pursuit of justice.

The second answer is the one we offer in this book and elaborate in greater theoretical detail in the companion volume. This is that policy makers and judges have increasingly turned away from mandating redistribution because it became evident that the mandates were futile and even self-defeating. In these pages, we attempt to describe why the mandates were futile. We argue that court-ordered desegregation treated schools as monopolies, in which policy makers could redistribute access to resources at will. This, we argue, was a basic misconception of the nature and function of the educational marketplace.

FAILURE OF WILL OR SELF-DEFEATING POLICY?

Gary Orfield is perhaps the most prominent of the many activists and scholars who argue that the failure to achieve true desegregation in our schools has been due to a failure of will in applying a racially oriented command and control approach to attendance in public schools. Orfield, heading advocacy projects at Harvard and later at UCLA, has consistently argued that resegregation from the 1980s onward occurred because the United States government did not have sufficient political will to aggressively push the redistribution of students, and that desegregation activists must come up with new strategies to pursue racial redistribution in the schools and in American society.[8]

Orfield's unflagging insistence on the necessity for judicial coercion led social scientists Stephan and Abigail Thernstrom to remark, in a May 2014 *Wall Street Journal* editorial, that "Mr. Orfield seemingly favors permanent court supervision over most school districts."[9] To be fair to Gary Orfield and other advocates of coercive desegregation, it is important to acknowledge the historical background to the command and control approach. The freedom of choice period before the time of more active governmental intervention, after all, was a time when districts simply maintained the de facto segregated schools that school officials had created.

One may question whether federal intervention into local school districts is still needed now that school boards have many elected members from racial and ethnic minorities. One may also wonder whether the revolution from above approach of having public policy dictated by federal judges and Department of Justice attorneys is consistent with the principles of a liberal democracy. But we will argue in this book that the race or ethnicity based redistribution of students simply does not work because it is contrary to the character of schools as marketplaces of educational resources.

In a command and control economy, the direction of the distribution of goods by a central authority leads to black market trading or to the flight of goods and people to freer markets. For similar reasons of self-interest, the command and control approach to school desegregation has produced evasive maneuvers by parents with different visions for their children's education than the government would impose upon them. Ignoring or misunderstanding the self-interest of families, especially families with the capacity to make their own market decisions, condemned efforts to equalize opportunity by redistributing students to failure.

SUMMARY OF THE BOOK

In the first chapter of this work, we describe the political economy of education and discuss how this is related to the goal of creating equality of educational opportunity. We begin with a theoretical discussion of the motivations for seeking this equality of opportunity. Many of the commonly recognized goals of education; such as preparing people for the job market, maintaining social order, or shaping informed citizens; do not necessitate equality in schooling. The primary justification for egalitarian outcomes for students is the view that people have the individual right to enter a competitive society at the same starting point.

The "level playing field" is a frequent way of expressing the need to provide equal chances for members of all categories, especially those who have been historically disadvantaged. However, we argue that education is essentially a market of exclusivity. Although pedagogical techniques, institutional organization, or material resources may contribute to educational value, the most important source of a good school is the clientele. Students from socially and economically advantaged backgrounds contribute more to the value of schools than funding does.

Chapter 2 discusses what the political economy of education means for schooling as a competitive market. In looking at the nature of the educational marketplace, we consider how governmental initiatives to redistribute resources can produce unintended consequences when those who have competitive advantages respond to those initiatives. Education is never really a monopoly. Therefore, redistribution encourages the haves to take their own resources to locations with better pay-offs, especially when those pay-offs involve the well-being of their own children.

Following the idea that educational value is largely created by the clientele, we establish that the student composition of schools is closely linked to the quality of school environments. Therefore, when authorities try to mandate equality of opportunity by redistributing students, the authorities lower the quality of school environments for those most able to make other choices in the educational marketplace. In the last part of chapter 2 we make this argument more concrete by discussing the school marketplace in practice.

Chapters 3 and 4 bring the theme of the school marketplace in practice down to the level of specific districts. Chapter 3 sketches case histories of districts around the nation in which ambitious attempts to redistribute students by race or ethnicity ended in districts or metropolitan areas that were entirely segregated. Chapter 4 then tries to identify a few districts that have been celebrated as desegregation success stories, or that might be seen as relatively successful in providing some opportunities to minority students through desegregation strategies.

We end chapter 4 by discussing the patterns underlying all of these districts. In all, we argue, the haves (consisting mainly of middle class and mainly of white families) sought to maximize the advantages of their own children, undermining attempts to redistribute advantages. When there were other places to go, the haves left the districts engaging in massive student redistribution. It was more difficult to leave some other districts, but even in these the pursuit of self-interest resulted in outcomes such as in-school segregation through tracking. Some disadvantaged minority students did benefit from access to better school environments, but these were always small proportions.

Chapter 5 examines the market-oriented reform programs that have begun to succeed school desegregation. Charter school and voucher programs emerged from the desegregation movement, and they continue to be influenced by it. Redistributing students by race had not created equal opportunity. Instead, it had left many predominantly minority districts, especially the poorest, more segregated than ever before. School choice offered a new possibility to frustrated minority districts. Since command and control redistribution had failed, policy makers and concerned citizens turned to subsidized choices instead.

The school choice movement inherited from desegregation an overriding concern with improving the schooling of the disadvantaged, especially among racial and ethnic minorities, in order to equalize opportunity. Therefore, as we point out in this chapter, charter schools and vouchers have been disproportionately oriented toward subsidizing choices for minority students. Looking at the locations we discussed in chapters 3 and 4, we detail how these market-oriented approaches spread rapidly around the nation.

The chapter looks, also, at how desegregation continues to haunt the debate over choice strategies. Many of the arguments over the consequences of charters and vouchers, in public and in the courts, continue to focus on how these kinds of subsidies affect student populations. Some maintain that school choice produces greater segregation, while others argue that it can lead to less segregated schools. We suggest that the desegregation heritage has distorted the debate, by directing attention away from the best ways to realistically provide the best education to all students.

Although some evidence does indicate that school choice can improve education for the most disadvantaged, we suggest that neither charter schools nor vouchers constitute a panacea. Choice will not eliminate racial and ethnic or socioeconomic achievement gaps. It will not provide an answer to the historic and socioeconomic forces that tend to segregate our society and the schools inside of it. We suggest that competition among schools, for good or ill, can actually increase inequality. Massive voucher subsidies, moreover, can become a new kind of redistribution, with all the problems and contradictions of subsidies in a competitive society and economy.

Chapter One

The Political Economy of Education and Equality of Educational Opportunity

WHY SEEK EQUALITY OF OPPORTUNITY IN EDUCATION?

The school desegregation movement was, above all else, an effort to establish equality of opportunity in education across racial and ethnic categories. Given the nation's long history of denying equal access to members of minority groups, especially African Americans, the desirability of this effort appears immediately obvious. However, in order to understand why coercive desegregation has failed at its goal, we can begin by thinking more closely about the purposes of education, about how these purposes are connected to equality of opportunity, and about what the educational marketplace means for attempts to equalize schooling.

If one were to ask people why we have public education, and why students should enjoy equal access to public education, one would receive a number of answers.[1] Some would point out that we need trained workers for our economy, and that the amount of training required of workers is continually rising. Therefore, we need to educate all potential workers, including those from families unable to bear the costs of schooling for their own children.

Other people would say that public instruction has "spillover" benefits (or "externalities," in economic jargon) beyond the purely economic. The "schools not jails" slogan is based on the view that schooling can lessen juvenile delinquency and divert people from criminal careers, precisely because it places them in socially useful jobs. Further, communities with good schools can attract business investment and people who can afford to be

1

homeowners, so that even residents who have no children will indirectly benefit from the availability of high-quality, public education.[2]

Still other people would answer that a democratic society cannot be successful without an educated citizenry, because it takes knowledgeable citizens to choose wise government leaders and participate in the processes of government.[3] Thomas Jefferson was an ardent proponent of the necessity of a broadly educated citizenry for the survival of the young American republic. None of these responses, not even Jefferson's, really addresses the question of equality, though.

If we are training future employees, then we need job-focused variety in the training, not equality. An economy needs people with different skills, who would receive differing levels of financial rewards even if the distribution of wealth and income were more equal than it is today. Some critics of the American educational system have attacked it for perpetuating the inequality of a capitalist society.[4] However, these critics ignore an indisputable, if uncomfortable fact: if we have public education in order to put people into existing jobs, then sorting people into unequal economic positions is exactly what public schools are supposed to do.

The response that education benefits the surrounding community also provides no justification for providing the same level of education to all students, or to all communities. During the term of President Richard M. Nixon, the president's education commissioner, Sidney Marland, Jr., appeared before the U.S. Congress to argue that what he saw as social disorder and alienation among American youth resulted from an educational system that was not closely linked to vocational and career training.[5] For Marland, the externality of social order would be a consequence of schools doing an efficient job of placing young people into appropriate jobs.

The view that education contributes to communities by attracting businesses and desirable residents not only provides no support for equality in education, but it implies that educational systems are part of the competition among communities and are therefore necessarily unequal. As the economist Charles Tiebout recognized, localities vie with each other for businesses and people.[6]

Although general prosperity can increase, at any given time a firm can choose to move either to one place or another; it cannot set up shop everywhere. Similarly, people who are valued local citizens can only own a finite number of homes, and for every place someone buys a home, there is another where that person will not buy a home. Many of the externalities of schooling, then, are matters of some districts being able to attract residents with differing abilities to contribute to schools.

To be an informed citizen, one must be able to read well, to think critically, and to discuss public issues. It may also be the case that citizens of a democracy need to have some common set of values, and that public education can be an effective way of instilling these values.[7] This would only be a claim that all citizens should share some basic educational foundation, though. A good education for all citizens is highly desirable, if it can be achieved, but there is no reason that all citizens need to be educated to the same level or in the same way.

An answer that most of us would give, and which would be much more relevant to the issue of equality in education, would be that education is an essential source of economic opportunity. It is, in other words, a resource that enables young people to compete for unequal positions in a market economy. This means that an education is, first, an economic good that people can use to obtain other economic goods. Second, education is a right of individuals, rather than a service to society as a whole.

The idea that education is an individual right to a basic social good has led to a long series of attempts at equalization in funding of schools over the course of the past half-century. If each American has a right to an education that will put all at the same starting point in a competitive economy, then it seems unjust and unreasonable that spending on some students is only a fraction of spending on others.

Even if, as we argue below in our examination of what makes an education valuable, school achievement is influenced more by the characteristics students bring from their neighborhoods and families to schools than it is by the books, buildings, and equipment of schools, this should not be an excuse for financially shortchanging the schools of the disadvantaged. Money is never irrelevant. But money isn't everything, either, especially with regard to producing positive academic outcomes.

The heritage of locally supported schools means that schools rely heavily on local tax revenues for their funding, primarily in the form of property taxes. Although federal elementary and secondary education funding has historically risen somewhat (from 6.1 percent of total funding in 1989–1990 to 12.7 percent in 2009–2010) and schools have consistently drawn from 40 percent to 50 percent of revenues from state sources, local property taxes alone have consistently accounted for over one-third of all the financial resources of schools.[8]

School districts located in relatively well-to-do communities can raise more tax dollars for schools than poorer communities can. Thus, locally controlled and supported schools in the United States have been highly unequal in the amount of money they spend on students. If one views equality of education as an individual right to a publicly provided resource for socioeconomic mobility, then redistribution of funds from more prosperous to less prosperous districts appears logical.

Seeing education in terms of the civil rights of individuals has led proponents of equalization of spending to pursue their goals through the court system, maintaining that students in districts that have relatively small revenues suffer a violation of legal rights. For example, plaintiffs in the *San Antonio v. Rodriguez* case in 1973 attempted to have the Texas system of financing schools declared unconstitutional.

Attorneys arguing against the Texas system of education financing claimed that different levels of funding for different school districts violated the Fourteenth Amendment's guarantee of equal protection under the law. However, the U.S. Supreme Court threw out the lower court's decision that the Texas system was unconstitutional, on the grounds that the U.S. Constitution offers no guarantees of education.

At the state level attempts to equalize spending have been somewhat more successful, and several state courts limited inequality in spending among their districts. Among the most notable was the *Serrano v. Priest* decision in California in 1971. In this case, the California Supreme Court ruled that spending among California school districts could not differ by more than one hundred dollars per student. Critics of court-ordered equalization have argued that such decisions led to a lowering of support for public schools, particularly among wealthier families who removed their children from public school systems altogether.

The author and educational critic Jonathan Kozol has linked the isolation of African American students in *de facto* segregated schools to the unequal distribution of funds across district lines in eloquent, persuasive, and moving terms. Describing the gap between predominantly white suburbs and predominantly black central cities in locations across the country, he points out that average per pupil spending in New York City in 1987 came to about $5,500 per pupil, while some New York suburban areas spent over $11,000 per student.

Kozol noted that in 1988 Detroit spent $3,600 yearly on each student, while nearby suburbs spent well over $6,000 on each of their pupils. In pages that everyone concerned about contemporary education should read, Kozol gives us vignettes of the desperately poor neighborhoods surrounding inner city schools, the lamentable conditions in those schools, and the struggles and aspirations of disadvantaged students and their families. Kozol expresses frustration that . . .

> the rigging of the game and the acceptance, which is nearly universal, of uneven playing fields reflect a dark unspoken sense that other people's children are of less inherent value than our own. Now and then, in private, affluent suburbanites concede that certain aspects of the game may be a trifle rigged to their advantage. "Sure, it's a bit unjust," they may concede, "but that's reality and that's the way the game is played. . . ."[9]

We share this frustration, and we agree that there is a deep contradiction between the belief that all Americans should be competing on an equal footing in a market economy that rewards the hardest working and most talented individuals, and the reality that people in our nation really do begin this competition with dramatically unequal preparation. It is even more frustrating and disturbing, given our centuries of slavery and legal discrimination, that the unequal starting points should be so closely associated with race and ethnicity.

Clearly, attempts to create equal opportunities through redistributing school funding are motivated by many of the same goals as attempts to equalize opportunities by distributing students among schools. Both are motivated by the belief that the benefits of public education, whether produced by the allocation of tax revenues or by the socioeconomic settings of schools, should be available, as a fundamental right, to all those preparing for life in our society.

Despite our discomfort with inequality of opportunity, we think that there may be a problem with seeing education as a "game" consisting of individual players who are all supposed to begin with the same chips, but that has been unfairly rigged in favor of some. In order to describe to readers why we believe this is a misleading picture of the way the political economy of education actually works, we want to begin with an examination of how the chips acquire their value in the first place, and then look at the nature of the game itself.

By looking closely at just what kind of economic good a public education really is, we can begin to understand what schools are selling, and what makes this "educational good" so desirable. Thinking about education in this light can help us see how redistributing students by race or by social class affects the value of what schools have to offer. In turn, we can see whether school desegregation, which is motivated by the same goals as equalization of funding, does actually make a desirable education more widely available.

WHAT MAKES AN EDUCATION VALUABLE?

In classical economic theory, goods are frequently assumed to have a relatively fixed utility for consumers. However, the market value of those goods can vary because supply and demand can affect marginal utility—the amount of satisfaction derived from each additional quantity of the good. As demand goes up, even though the utility remains the same, the marginal utility increases because there are more potential consumers desiring the good.

However, some economists recognize that utility may not be fixed and that utility (and not just marginal utility) may be created by consumption. The more people who want the latest Xbox 360 video game or smart phone, the more people there are who want these things precisely because other people want them. The utility of a good can also be established not simply by how many people want it, but by which people want it. This is the exclusivity factor, an economic fact pointed out by Thorstein Veblen, who coined the term "conspicuous consumption."[10]

Exclusivity can create utility in two ways: First, the "snob appeal" of a good can contribute to its utility. Second, some types of goods are substantially shaped by their consumption. An example of this would be the neighborhood as a commodity. Arguably, one of the reasons that wealthy neighborhoods are nice places to live is that people who live in them (the consumers) have the money to make them nice places to live. The other consumers are a big part of what is being sold.

We propose that schools may be seen as commodities that depend heavily on who consumes them (the students) for their utility—their quality of intrinsic desirability. The implication is that it is difficult to redistribute or equalize educational experiences because some degree of exclusivity is part of the value of those experiences. Why, after all, do Harvard and Princeton boast their very low acceptance rates?

Higher achievement scores and higher socioeconomic status of student bodies raise the "marginal utility" of an educational institution—lower scores and lower status students lower the "marginal utility." Thus, schools populated by low achieving, low socioeconomic status students have lower "value" for consumers who are "shopping" for educational value. And consumers of education do indeed shop. There's more than a grain of truth in the following description by humorist and Pulitzer Prize winner Dave Barry about education-obsessed New Yorkers' search for the best possible schools for their children:

> "Serious parents start obsessing about Harvard before their child is, technically, born. They spend their evenings shouting the algebraic equations in the general direction of the womb so the child will have an edge during the intensely competitive process of applying for New York City's exclusive private preschools—yes, PREschools—where tuition can run—and I am not making this figure up—well over $15,000 a year."[11]

That was ten years ago. In 2014, an exclusive New York nursery school could cost $40,000 a year, and elite private schools are in such demand on Manhattan that one school's acceptance rate for unconnected families was only 2.4 percent.[12] Many competitive New York parents no longer even consider these outrageous prices in their search for the best school for their children, and are willing to pay special consulting firms up to $21,500 just to "give them a leg up" in the cut-throat admissions process.[13]

MORE THAN MONEY

What makes a pre-school worth $40,000 a year? It is probably not the building that houses the program, regardless how ritzy. Rather, we believe, this price includes the privilege of attending school with the sons and daughters of New York City's most socioeconomically advantaged students. This view, that the students create the value of their education for each other, is a logical extension of ideas that are widely accepted among educational economists. Eric Hanushek, in one of the most widely cited studies of the influences on student performance, concluded in 1986 that "there appears to be no strong or systematic relationship between school expenditures and student performance."[14] We can take student performance as an indicator of what students have learned and the skills that they have acquired: in other words, of the "utility" of education. What students know and can do can be understood as the product of schooling.

While Hanushek's findings became "the prevailing view among economists who study school resources and academic achievement,"[15] they have been questioned by school administrators and others who have maintained that spending on education can be an important part of improving education. The issue of how much money matters and how it can be spent most effectively is an important one. Certainly no one, including Hanushek, has claimed that educational spending is completely irrelevant and that we should spend nothing at all on schooling.

Even those who maintain that current forms of spending have a significant effect on educational performance rarely argue that spending is the only influence on academic achievement. The questions of how much money should be invested in schools and how the money should be spent are important ones, from the perspective of a public official. But if we look at the matter from the point of view of a consumer of education—a family making decisions about its own children—the issue is not whether money makes any difference at all, but what makes the most difference in determining whether a school is "good."

As a rule, much more federal money is targeted to predominately minority than predominantly white schools. Yet, these billions of dollars have in general not made these schools significantly more attractive to middle-class students. In our earlier research into desegregating schools in Louisiana, we found fairly typical examples in two technologically advanced schools in the school district of Lafayette.

One was a 90 percent African American school, populated almost entirely with at-risk, high poverty students, located in a new, modern facility incorporating all of the most modern educational and technological innovations available. The school was well-known for its disorder, unsatisfied faculty, and abysmally low student performance. Parents were not breaking down the doors to get their children into this school with the latest facilities. Instead, the school had a problem filling its classrooms to capacity.

The same district was home to an even newer, more technologically advanced majority black school ordered built by a judge in the name of desegregation (though the school couldn't attract a 50 percent white student body). One of the authors was told of so many resources flooding into the school that teachers and administrators did not know what to do with them all.[16] These resources included a room full of brand new pianos, a dance studio, and a cutting edge computer lab. None of this helped improve student academic achievement.

In a few desegregation cases, the amount spent has been nothing short of phenomenal, though it still wasn't enough to attract middle-class students. For example, as a consequence of the 1996 court-approved consent degree in East Baton Rouge Parish, Louisiana, $27 million was subsequently spent on desegregation efforts, including the establishment of "equity" accounts for historically black schools. So much money was flowing into these schools that the superintendent at the time declared, "The principals are telling me they're finding it difficult to decide what else they need beyond what they've already bought."[17]

The Baton Rouge equity spending paled in comparison to the funds ordered spent in the desegregating Kansas City, Missouri, School District (KCMSD) to help close the black-white achievement gap, and attract white students. In *Jenkins v. Missouri*,[18] the district court judge's directive to the KCMSD to spend $2 billion over a 12-year period was upheld by the United States Supreme Court.[19] Since the local district was virtually bankrupt due to white flight and the failure of voters to pass school tax increases, the federal judge held the state partially liable for both the segregated school system and the cost to fix it.

The federal judge ordered that local property taxes be doubled, and imposed an income tax surcharge on all those working in Kansas City but living elsewhere. The high court ruled that such draconian measures were constitutional and necessary to overcome state sponsored segregation. According to a very thorough Cato Institute policy analysis of the KCMSD desegregation spending program . . .

> Kansas City spent as much as $11,700 per pupil—more money per pupil, on a cost of living adjusted basis, than any other of the 280 largest districts in the country. The money bought higher teachers' salaries, 15 new schools, and such amenities as an Olympic-sized swimming pool with an underwater viewing room, television and animation studios, a robotics lab, a 25-acre wildlife sanctuary, a zoo, a model United Nations with simultaneous translation capability, and field trips to Mexico and Senegal. The student-teacher ratio was 12 or 13 to 1, the lowest of any major school district in the country.[20]

In the ensuing twelve years, white flight continued. During that time, black achievement remained low, and the black-white achievement gap had not been reduced. Even the original federal court judge on the case had to admit that the massive spending had made little difference in school achievement, and that the district had done everything in its power to undo vestiges of past de jure segregation. [21]

In *Missouri v. Jenkins II* the U.S. Supreme Court ultimately restricted the federal court's far-reaching powers in the case. The high court questioned the efficacy of spending almost $200 million per year on desegregation remedies in a district with ultimately fewer than 36,000 students. Further, the court ruled it was unconstitutional to use state funds to raise KCMSD teacher salaries to higher levels than the surrounding districts. [22]

Jenkins II also ruled that the district did not have to raise minority achievement scores to the national average to meet the "quality of education" desegregation target. The district only had to undo that part of the black-white achievement gap caused by previous de jure segregation. The Supreme Court reiterated the criteria it established in its 1971 *Swann* decision that any desegregation remedy, "must be designed as nearly as possible to restore the victims of discriminatory conduct to the position they would have occupied in the absence of such conduct."

It is certainly beyond the realm of science how one could ever calculate the number of points on a nationally-normed test pre-*Brown* discrimination cost blacks in KCMSD. It is apparently not beyond the legal realm, though. The system was declared unitary in 2003 after the new judge on the case ruled that the black-white achievement gap had been sufficiently reduced to finally undo all vestiges of past de jure segregation. [23]

The exorbitant spending in the KCMSD was not just targeted at raising black achievement levels, but at stemming white flight by making the schools more attractive. The Cato Institute estimated that it cost Kansas City about $500,000 in spending for each white student it attracted. Perhaps the district could have attracted more by paying their families directly, but buying student attendance so straightforwardly would clearly have been unacceptable.

It is possible that the ultimate test of the hypothesis that pouring in money can raise the educational achievement of a high needs district (and attract the middle class to underperforming schools) was carried out in the Roosevelt School District on Long Island. The state of New York took over this one square mile district, with only 2,700 students in 2002, and embarked upon what may have been the greatest per pupil spending binge in U.S. history to raise the achievement of the low income African American and Latino/Hispanic students who made up most of Roosevelt's school population.

By the time the spending splurge in the Roosevelt district ended in 2013, New York state taxpayers had pumped $245.5 million into the tiny district, which only boasted one high school that had an enrollment of only 800 students.[24] At the beginning of this government experiment, an assembly-woman who represented the district was quoted as saying, "This is a new era. This is a win-win for everyone, for the children, the parents, the taxpayers, the residents of the state . . . we should begin to see an immediate turn-around."[25] A state senator more soberly observed that "The proof is going to be in the scores." [26]

The spending included a whopping $66.9 million high school renovation project to create a state-of-the-art building. By the opening of school in September 2013, the authors conservatively estimated that the Roosevelt School District had spent an average of 30 percent more per pupil than even Kansas City had invested in its largely ineffective educational spending spree, after adjusting for inflation. In 2011–2012, the district reported spend-ing a total average of $31,551 per student. This compared to a total average of $20,410 for all school districts in New York State,[27] and a 2011 national average per pupil expenditure of $10,560.

What are the results of Roosevelt's mini-experiment in exorbitant spend-ing? According to the 2012 New York State Report Cards, there has been only very modest improvement in Roosevelt's test scores, and the high school remains on the list of the state's lowest scholastic performers (those in the bottom 5 percent). The district had met very few of its Average Yearly Progress goals, and the graduation rate was only 62 percent, compared to a state average of 80 percent.[28] Moreover, not even one white or Asian student had been attracted to the high-spending district. The assemblywoman who represents the residents in the Roosevelt district proclaimed at the beginning of the state takeover in 2002 that "we should see an immediate turnaround" in the district's schools. In 2013, that same assemblywoman sponsored legis-lation to extend the state's control of the district.[29] The district's residents were still waiting for the promised turnaround.

Contrast the scenarios above with the case of Benjamin Franklin High School in New Orleans. The school for gifted students was housed for years in an old, dilapidated building with no air-conditioning (it has long since moved to a much better building). Yet, while housed in its decaying urban digs, Franklin traditionally produced either the highest or very nearly the highest performing students in the entire state of Louisiana, with parents clamoring to get their children admitted.

When the state took over the failing schools of New Orleans after Hurri-cane Katrina at the end of 2005, leaving only the top performing schools under the control of the local school district, the highly selective Benjamin Franklin High School remained one of the few under the administration of the Orleans Parish School Board. Although its already limited physical re-sources had been diminished by the storm, it was still the only high school in the district to receive an "A" on the school report card issued by the state as recently as 2013.[30]

Clearly, exorbitant spending didn't help in making the Kansas City, Missouri School District more attractive to the middle class. A substandard building didn't deter parents from fighting to get their children into Benjamin Franklin. What about Benjamin Franklin High, then, made it so attractive? The evidence suggests that it was the clientele.

IT'S THE CLIENTELE

A view that stretches back at least to James S. Coleman's pioneering work on academic achievement in the 1960s is that the single greatest influence on student performance is the family background of all the students in the school. Our own research has supported this view.[31] Education is a social process, not just information that books and teachers pour into the heads of students.

Students learn from those they interact with all day long, and the people they are around most often are other students. If the other students come from homes with well-educated parents who place a premium on books that they read to their children, then these students bring these educational assets with them to school. The more students in a school who bring such assets, the better the school can educate all students.

Parents make choices about the educations of their children. They choose some public schools over others by moving into neighborhoods that they believe have good schools. They choose magnet programs or schools with special offerings by seeking out these opportunities within public schools. If they believe it is in the best interests of their children and they can afford to do so (or sometimes even if they can't afford to do so[32]), they choose private schools, like the competitive New York parents who'll spend $40,000 a year on their pre-schoolers.

When parents make choices about education, they are taking part in an educational economy. As one writer on educational economy has observed, "economic agents are utility maximizers. Every time we make a choice, we select the alternative that yields the greatest utility, subject to the resources available. . . . Education exists because it provides utility. If it did not, there would be no demand for it."[33]

Regardless of how great or little a part funding for schools plays in the quality of education, schoolmates with educational advantages are the most important influence on educational quality. When parents try to put their children into the best schools they can afford, whether they realize it or not, they are placing their children with the most advantaged schoolmates they

can afford. There is, unfortunately, a clear correlation between the educational advantages of schoolmates and the race/ethnicity of schoolmates.

The American history of racial and ethnic inequality has left us with a
substantial achievement gap between whites and Asians on the one hand, and
black and Hispanic students on the other. This means that the racial composition of a school is still a big part of what determines the utility of the school.
It is not simply that a school's racial makeup is connected to how well the
school does overall. It is also connected to the educational benefits individual
students receive from their schools.

Now, the reader will note that in the passage of the educational economist
we just cited there are two influences on choice: "the greatest utility" and
"resources available." Without governmental attempts at redistribution, those
who have the greatest resources can obtain the best educations. The financial
resources of families are closely related to the individual educational advantages of children (children from fairly well-to-do families are the most likely
to have college-educated parents and high educational aspirations).

Those who can afford good educations will send their children to school
with children from other families that can afford good educations. Although
financial resources and educational advantages are related, they are not the
same thing. Most college towns have good schools where faculty, comfortable but rarely wealthy, concentrate their own children. In this case, though,
the "resources" consist of being in a location with many educationally advantaged people.

Why do schools with educationally advantaged students also tend to be
better funded than schools with the less advantaged? People put their money
where they put their children. In a sense, other people's children *are* of less
inherent value than our own, at least to us. If we valued all children as much
as we value our own, we would treat our own exactly as we treat every other
child. ("Sorry, Mary, no college fund for you. We're distributing all of our
savings equally among all children in our county.")

Whether this is the way people should behave is debatable. We would
argue that those who give no preference to their own wards or offspring are,
to put it bluntly, bad parents. Even if we are wrong about this, though, most
people do put their efforts, their emotions, and their money into the well-
being of their own families. But we suspect we are not wrong. The tendency
of parents to promote the well-being of their own children contributes to
inequality. It also has benefits, though.

Many years ago the economist Adam Smith recognized the utility of
individual self-interest for the larger good of society.[34] Whereas twisted self-
interest run amuck can lead to selfish actions that hurt others, it would seem
that Smith's "invisible hand" principle is particularly germane to parental
self-interest in rearing well-educated children. It's hard to disagree that, all

things being equal, contributing well-educated children to society is more beneficial to us all than contributing poorly educated offspring.

One might argue that this tendency for families to invest in their own children, more than in the children of others, is a good reason to try to redistribute students. By putting children of privilege in schools with children of those who have suffered historical deprivation and discrimination, we not only spread the assets of educational preparation more widely, we also encourage those who can invest in education to put their resources into schools that serve students from all backgrounds.

The attempt to redistribute family social resources by redistributing students was the central idea behind school desegregation. This might have worked if school systems were monopolies. The reality is that school systems are competitive marketplaces that can exercise the least control over the choices of those with the greatest available resources. This fact requires that we look more closely at schooling as a unique kind of market.

CHAPTER SUMMARY

This chapter has identified the quest for equality of educational opportunity as the fundamental goal of the school desegregation movement. Rather than accept the desirability of equality of opportunity as an unexamined assumption, the chapter has considered the purposes of education. Schooling can prepare individuals for needed positions in the workforce. It can promote social order and contribute to community life. It can advance civic participation by creating an informed citizenry.

None of these societal purposes of education requires equality in education. In fact, preparing people for different needed jobs may involve educating people unequally. The main argument for equality in education comes from the civil rights view that education entails the right of all individuals, regardless of race or background, to begin at the same starting point as all other individuals in a competitive marketplace. This civil rights perspective on education confronts the painful reality that people of different races and from different socioeconomic backgrounds enter our competitive society with vastly unequal levels of preparation.

In order to look at why this educational inequality exists, the chapter has looked briefly at what makes an education valuable. Although schools do need money, the evidence does not support the argument that some schools are better than others simply because some are better funded. Instead, the main determinant of educational value is the clientele. While there are many influences on the quality of schooling, the most important one is the clientele. Good schools generally concentrate students who come from advantaged backgrounds and bad schools generally concentrate students from disadvantaged backgrounds.

The most basic problem with seeking greater equality of opportunity in education, then, is that education is a market of exclusivity. Families with financial and social resources to invest in their own children maximize these resources by choosing to place their children in institutions attended by other children from families with financial and social resources. The next chapter will investigate this idea in greater depth by examining how education works as a marketplace of exclusivity and what this has meant for monopolistic attempts to redistribute opportunity through school desegregation.

Chapter Two

Schooling as a Competitive Market

THE EDUCATIONAL MARKETPLACE

The greatest problem for any controlled economy is the existence of alternative markets. If there are two neighboring cities and one limits the profits of property owners through controlled rents, while the other allows property owners to maximize their profits by charging whatever the market will bear, then those who can readily transfer their funds will tend to shift investment out of the controlled market and into the uncontrolled one. This may be offset by special cultural characteristics of the one with controlled rents or by the difficulty in moving money from one place to another.

The city with the controlled rents would have the advantage of relatively cheap rents. These may not be attractive to investors, but they would certainly be attractive to renters, especially renters with limited incomes. With little investment and plenty of low-income inhabitants, housing would be tight and unappealing to upper income residents, who would be better able to afford the higher rent costs in the uncontrolled city. One of our two cities would eventually consist of deteriorating neighborhoods inhabited by the poor, while the other would become a bastion of affluence and upper-end employment.

Of course, reality is more complex than this. If the city with controls did have some especially desirable qualities, the controls might simply encourage people to transform rental housing into owner-occupied housing, driving out those who could not afford to buy their own homes. Or, the city might develop into pockets of comfortable owner-occupied neighborhoods and clusters of low-rent neighborhoods. In looking at possible consequences of attempts to control an economy, we always have to understand how people with differing abilities to choose will respond to those attempts in varied settings.

Turning from the example of cities to schools, we can ask what kinds of educational alternatives are available to families. To begin with, the United States has both public and private systems of education. Neither of these is free. Public education is funded through local property and sales taxes, state money, and federal money. The greatest single source of revenue for most districts comes from the local taxes that voters impose on themselves.

One relevant question is why some localities will tax themselves at higher rates than others, and we will discuss this (and what it means) shortly. But if public education is not free, its costs are at least relatively widespread and all property owners pay these costs, whether or not they have children in public schools. So why would anyone choose to pay tuition for a private school? Quite simply, they must be getting something they believe they will not get in a public school, and this something must be worth the additional cost to them—indeed, huge costs of as much as $40,000 a year per child for pre-school alone.

There is a substantial literature that indicates that private schools do a better job of educating students than public schools do.[1] While this is not accepted by all researchers, "research has consistently found that, even after controlling for selection effects, private-school students are more likely to graduate high school, attend college, attend a selective college, and graduate from college."[2] In addition, many parents may choose parochial or other religious schools because these teach or reinforce the beliefs and values they want their children to receive.

So, the question now becomes: why don't all parents send their children to private schools? If these are apparently better than public schools, and if all parents want to give the best possible education to their children, then why don't families abandon public schools altogether? Going back to the example of the two cities, one of the reasons people might choose to live in the controlled city, apart from the cheap rents, could be some special cultural characteristic of that city. Similarly, many parents will avoid religiously affiliated private schools precisely because they do not share the schools' beliefs and do not want those taught to their children.

Another reason families choose public schools is that sometimes these might really be the best choices. Private schools may, on average, show better results than public schools, but this does not mean that all private schools are better than all public schools. In many places, the local public school may be the best educational institution around, like the aforementioned Benjamin Franklin gifted high school in New Orleans, or the much sought after Bronx High School of Science in New York.

Even when a private school does appear to be a somewhat better choice than the public, the family needs to consider whether it is worth the extra expenditure, given the other demands on income and long-range plans for children. The more affluent the family is, the less of a sacrifice it will have to make for even small added benefits from private schooling. Additionally, parents who are highly educated are likely to place a great deal of value on any extra educational advantages and will be more willing to make sacrifices, sometimes huge ones, to obtain those advantages.

It is not at all surprising, then, that studies have consistently found that the affluent and well-educated parents are the most likely to send their children to private schools.[3] Those who have greater incomes can, of course, purchase more goods and more expensive goods. But even those with relatively high incomes make choices about spending. They do have a choice between, say, a new car and private school tuition that poorer people do not have. But we still need to ask why they choose the tuition.

The children from upper middle class or affluent families who had incomes at least three times greater than the poverty level made up almost two-thirds of the children in private schools in 2000, although just 42 percent of school children lived in these families. By contrast, children from families below the poverty line made up only 8 percent of all the students in private schools, including parochial schools intended to serve low-income neighborhoods.[4] Not only were the well-to-do more likely to spend their money on private education, private schools were good places to find other children from equally advantageous economic backgrounds.

In addition, given the connection between socioeconomic status and race in our country, it is also not surprising that most private school students are white, and not surprising that the affluent are heavily overrepresented in private schools. Our estimates from the 2012 American Community Survey indicate that 78 percent of the nation's private school students were white in that year, despite the fact that this group made up 68 percent of all the American children enrolled in kindergarten through twelfth grade, and 67 percent of public school students. Hispanic students, who made up about 23 percent of all pupils, were only 12 percent of non-public school students.

Blacks, who made up about 15 percent of American students in 2012, constituted just 9 percent of those in private schools.[5] Private schools were, understandably, primarily the domain of those who were relatively well off. Although individuals with incomes five times the poverty level or more were just 18 percent of the total kindergarten through 12th grade population, over 34 percent of the students in private schools came from these affluent families. Keeping in mind, again, that this includes parochial schools established in minority neighborhoods, we see that non-public schools in our country are overwhelmingly white and upper middle class.

Could these figures just be a reflection of the fact that people who have more money can afford to send their children to more expensive schools, and whites tend to have more money? That is undeniably part of the explanation.

Again, though, even people with money have to decide that it is better to spend it in one way than in another, and their decisions may depend on their settings and opportunities.

If the opportunities available in public schools are related to the racial compositions of schools, then we would expect the decisions of the relatively affluent (who have the most power to make decisions) to be affected by the racial make-up of the schools around them. That is precisely what we see. When people with higher incomes live in areas with large disadvantaged minority populations in the schools, they are more likely to turn to private education.

Figure 2.1 employs data from the 2010 and 2011 American Community Surveys of the U.S. Census. It examines whether those who can afford private schools are more likely to make this choice in locations with relatively large minority populations in the public schools. As this figure illustrates, in metropolitan areas where black and Hispanic students constituted up to one-third of all public school students, 29.8 percent of students from relatively affluent families and 30.7 percent of white students from well-off families attended private, rather than public schools.

In metropolitan areas with over one-third minority public school students, 39.8 percent of the well-off and 42.6 percent of the white well-off were choosing the more expensive option of private education. Members of the upper middle class in general, and specifically the white upper middle class clearly had more motivation to opt out of public schools in places where minorities were heavily represented in the public schools. High income enables people to choose private education but it does not explain why they do so.

As we look at historical events, in the next chapter, we will see that there are other factors that influence whether those with high levels of financial and social resources decide to invest in local public schools or look elsewhere. These metropolitan-level data give us only a rough indication of one influence on the economic decision-making of families. One can see the racial make-up of schools as part of the calculus used to make choices about schooling by those able to make choices.

From the 1970s onward, the nation's minority population grew dramatically, especially in the school-age population. As a result, more American young people were in places that contained many students from historically disadvantaged minority groups. To fully understand what this meant for schooling in America, we will need to look at what actually happened in particular school districts in the next two chapters. Thinking about schools as marketplaces, though, can help us grasp why the events in these districts unfolded as they did.

In the hypothetical example of the two cities that we gave above, we can consider what would happen as the low-income population of one expands in

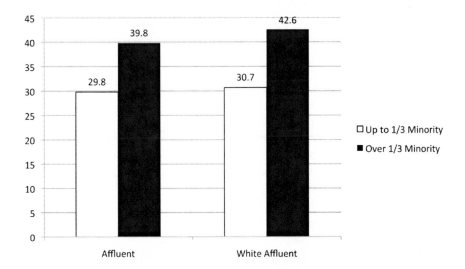

Figure 2.1. Percentages of Students from Relatively Affluent* Families and White Students from Relatively Affluent Families Attending Private Schools, by Metropolitan Minority Student Population, 2010-2011. *Defined as having family incomes five times the poverty level or more. *Source:* **2010-2011 American Community Survey data, Steven Ruggles, J. Trent Alexander, Katie Genadek, Ronald Goeken, Matthew B. Schroeder, and Matthew Sobek. Integrated Public Use Microdata Series: Version 5.0 [Machine-readable database] (Minneapolis: University of Minnesota, 2010).**

response to affordable rents. The residents with higher incomes could respond by buying property in special gated communities that, in essence, charge a membership fee for moving in. Some might choose these kinds of communities in any case, but more would be willing to pay these higher costs as the neighborhoods around them become more undesirable.

Why would the cheaper neighborhoods become less desirable? Because, to a large extent, the value of neighborhoods is established by exclusivity. To put it simply, most people do not want to live in low-income neighborhoods. Aside from the social problems generally associated with poverty, poor people have less money for the upkeep of homes and neighborhoods.

Turning back to schools as commodities, like homes, we can see why having large numbers of minority students as consumers of public schooling might put public schools at a competitive disadvantage. There is a large racial and ethnic achievement gap. The desirability of a school is, in large part, a product of its general level of achievement.

As minority enrollments go up, average achievement levels go down. We are not suggesting that every single school with high minority enrollments will have low achievement levels. We are also not minimizing the accomplishments of minority students who overcome the odds and surpass all others, including those who have much greater opportunities.

We are observing that an achievement gap associated with race or ethnicity necessarily means that heavy minority enrollments do lead to lower overall performance of schools. It is axiomatic: When the overall performance of public schools goes down, the incentive to pay extra costs for private schools goes up. Given this incentive, those who can do so will pay these extra costs.

Private schools are not the only competitors of public school systems, though. Each public school district also competes with other districts. We Americans often think of our system of public education as simply serving those who happen to live in a given place. But we are a highly mobile people, constantly moving, and constantly searching for new and better homes. Even when an American family moves to a location for a job, the automobile or mass transit means that mothers and fathers do not have to live where they work.

It has become routine for middle-class people, with children, who are newly arrived in a city or town to inquire first about the quality of schools in different areas before deciding where to settle. A parent in Scottsdale, Arizona, objecting to a school board plan to change attendance zones, put it succinctly in a letter to a local newspaper: "no family moves into a neighborhood without inquiring about the schools."[6] Any real estate agent will also attest to the fact that schools are the first consideration of home-seekers with children.

Competition among schools, then, can be competition between private and public schools for students, but it can also be competition among communities around school districts. This is the reason that researchers have found that housing prices are higher in public school districts that have high reported levels of student achievement.[7] A high quality school tends to draw home-seekers with children into its boundaries, driving up home prices. In effect, those who purchase or rent homes in order to be in a desirable school district are paying tuition in the form of higher mortgages or rents than they would pay if they lived elsewhere.

Many residents pay a second type of hidden tuition, in addition to housing costs in good school districts. The automobile has made it possible to live farther from one's place of employment, but distance also means expenditure of time and money on travel. If all schools in all places were of equal value, then a big motivation for commuting would be removed. In the course of our research, we spoke with one parent in the New Orleans area who had chosen to live across Louisiana's broad Lake Pontchartrain from his place of employment and spent at least an hour in traffic each day. Echoing the sentiments of many other commuters, he lamented,

I'd have to say that the schools were the number one factor in why we bought our house out here. I wish I didn't have to commute all the way across the bridge [the 24-mile causeway] to go to work every day. But the schools in New Orleans are a nightmare. I couldn't put my kids in one of those places.[8]

At this point, we come very close to our example of the two cities. When the value of one location goes down, those who can afford to do so look for other places to live. If artificially low rents or subsidized housing draw the poor into one community, then the members of the middle class will be willing to pay higher costs to live elsewhere.

The city with controlled or subsidized housing costs may have previously had a great deal of economic inequality, divided into rich and poor neighborhoods. When controls are introduced to allow the poor to live wherever they choose, this may appear to be a good way to create equity. The problem, though, is that the non-poor will simply move farther away. Similarly, when policies enable large numbers of relatively low performing students to enter a school, the families of higher performing students begin to move away.

So every public school must compete with both private schools and all other public schools that law and distance would allow prospective students to attend. What influences the choices that families make among these competing possibilities? The first answer, of course, remains the quality of education available in any one institution or system. The quality of education, it should be remembered, is largely a function of the other students, so that those who can make choices will always tend to choose to move away from the educationally disadvantaged and toward the advantaged.

As in the case of private vs. public schools, though, cost is still an issue. The greater the benefit a family gains from moving or paying a high mortgage or paying tuition, the more it will be willing to make the sacrifice. If we think of cost as what a family has to give up, then it is clear that a big mortgage payment costs a high-income family much less, as a share of its total resources, than it costs a relatively low-income family.

The availability of alternatives is also a part of the calculation. If a region has few highly regarded private schools, then settling in a neighborhood with a good public school may look like the more desirable option. If a family lives in a small city surrounded by comparatively deprived rural schools, then it can either accept the local public schools as they are or take whatever private schools may be available (or home-school their children, an increasingly popular option).

From the economic perspective that we are suggesting, a claim that "desegregation causes white flight" may be true, but overly simplistic. Where there are educationally exclusive public school areas, those who can afford to do so will move into those areas. When these public schools can compete effectively with private institutions, private schools tend to attract a relatively small proportion of those who can exercise choices, unless strong religious belief or some other cultural preference gives the edge to a private school.

The existence of private and competing public schools makes it difficult to establish monopolistic control over any school system. But the complexity of the educational marketplace encompasses more than these two forms of competition. Choices inside of schools also exist. According to the National Center for Education Statistics, in the 2011–2012 academic year, 56 percent of public high schools had advanced placement programs.[9] During the 2003–2004 school year, 69 percent of U.S. public schools offered gifted and talented or honors programs, by definition highly selective.[10]

These kinds of special programs provide opportunities for an elite, exclusive education within public schools. They also long tended to be segregated by race and class. A study of eighth graders based on the 1988 National Educational Longitudinal Study found that white students made up 82 percent of the students classified as gifted, although they made up only 71 percent of the total student population at the time of the study.[11]

In 2009, black students were fewer than 9 percent of those who earned advanced placement credit, while the much smaller Asian student population accounted for over 11 percent of all those earning AP credit.[12] Since the classification of students as "advanced placement," "honors," or "gifted and talented" is based largely on achievement measured through test scores, the test score gap between white and disadvantaged minority students means that classroom segregation inside of schools is generally a result of such programs or other kinds of tracking based on academic achievement.

We should consider, then, how attempts at desegregation tend to affect the educational marketplace, considering that the "product" is the quality of education. First, the effect of redistributing students depends on how many students will be redistributed and on how great the gap is between the advantaged and the disadvantaged. If there is no achievement gap at all between students from different racial groups, redistribution will not affect the product at all. If this were the case, though, there would be no justification for desegregation in the first place.

If only a few students from historically disadvantaged groups enter schools with members of advantaged groups, this should have a fairly small impact on the quality of education. Thinking about our imperfect example of the city, if controls, subsidies, or other means of housing assistance bring a single low-income family into a neighborhood, this may have relatively little impact on the community. Districts with large minority populations who have much greater educational disadvantages than students from the national majority pose the greatest problem.

If the city consists almost entirely of middle to upper income people (admittedly an unlikely scenario), then it may be possible to scatter all the disadvantaged in good neighborhoods without much of a change. If, on the other hand, the city consists primarily of the economically disadvantaged surrounding small pockets of affluence, then the quality of life in affluent neighborhoods could be seriously threatened by their opening to the poor. The more this quality of life declines, the greater the motivation of the affluent to leave for somewhere else.

Next, if we consider how desegregation affects choices, this depends on the resources of those making the choices. The most well-to-do families will have the least difficulty in moving to private schools, if there is even a small decline in the desirability of public schools. If public schooling declines greatly, perhaps as a result of the entry of large numbers of students with significant educational disadvantages into previously elite institutions, then middle-class families will be willing to move or make other sacrifices in order to find high quality schooling.

Finally, the choices that families make depend on what choices are available to them, in addition to their resources. If there is a well-established set of private schools or a parochial school system, private education is a possibility for those with sufficient resources. If there are suburbs within driving distance, then resettlement in the suburbs may be an option. When the decline in overall school quality is not so serious that the educationally advantaged want to avoid desegregating schools altogether, special programs inside of schools, which offer exclusive schooling within apparently egalitarian settings, may become attractive.

One clear implication of this economic perspective on educational quality is that the tendency of schools to "sort" themselves according to race and socioeconomic status is not just "a 'taste for dissociation,' or the desire to be apart from people of a different race."[13] If it is true that states with racially diverse populations have more school districts than states with little diversity,[14] this is only partly a result of desires of people to associate with people like themselves or of prejudice against people different from themselves. More importantly, the sorting is largely produced by each family's search for the best available schooling it can afford.

As we look in the following two chapters at events in a wide sampling of desegregating school districts, readers should pay attention to how this model of schools as educational marketplaces can be used to understand what has happened in different districts around the country. Before looking at these school districts, though, we will look briefly at the evidence concerning why minority-dominated schools tend to have less advantageous environments for all students. Then, we will consider what this means for equality of educational opportunity.

SCHOOL COMPOSITION AND EDUCATIONAL ENVIRONMENTS

Throughout our research, we have consistently found that parental involvement in schools is critical to shaping educational environments. Parent groups can raise large sums of money to fund school activities, funnel donated computers and technology to under-equipped schools, and provide a pool of chaperones to accompany school field trips. All pupils benefit from having adults contribute time, resources, and attention, not just the children of those parents.

Beyond the material benefits to schools, parental involvement can also help create good schools by establishing communication between parents and teachers. A survey that we distributed among teachers in a school district in 1996 (the results of which we reported in an earlier book[15]) showed that teachers felt that parental involvement was essential to maintaining a constructive social environment. One teacher volunteered the observation that "discipline problems in my school stem from the fact that parents just aren't involved."[16]

Figure 2.2 shows three measures of active parental involvement for white, black, and Hispanic families. Taken from data for the National Center for Educational Statistics, this shows us percentages of parents in 2011–2012 who had ever attended an event, done volunteer or committee work, or participated in funding in a child's school during the previous year. There are clear differences among the parents of the groups included here.

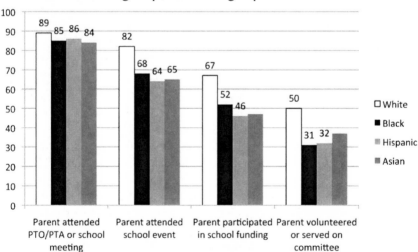

Figure 2.2. Active Parental Involvement in Schools, by Race and Ethnicity, 2011-12. *Source*: **U.S. Department of Education, National Center for Education Statistics, Parent and Family Involvement in Education Survey of the National Household Education Surveys Program (NHES), 2012.**

Nearly three-quarters (82 percent) of white parents had attended a school event, compared to 68 percent of black parents, and only 64 percent of Hispanic parents. As for participating in school funding, the pattern was the same: white parents again lead the pack, with Hispanic parents trailing all other groups. Doing volunteer work in a school or serving on a school committee shows a greater level of involvement than merely attending an event, so the percentages for this third measure are understandably smaller than those for the first two.

A little under half (43 percent) of white parents had done some kind of service work in schools. By contrast, though, only slightly over a quarter of black parents and slightly under a quarter of Hispanic parents had been volunteers. While parents can be important for educational environments, these are created most directly by the students themselves. The obvious implication of these statistics is that schools dominated by minority students will have fewer parental volunteers than schools with mostly white students.

A social order conducive to learning is essential to the environment of any school. Unfortunately, social order is also correlated with racial and ethnic compositions. Figure 2.3 shows percentages of black, Hispanic, Asian, and white students in grades 6 through 12 in 2007 that had been suspended or expelled from school.

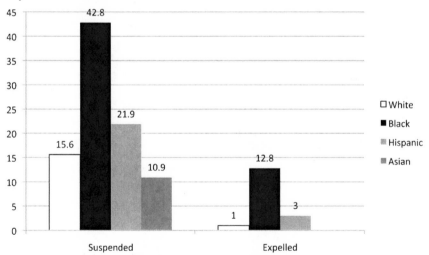

Figure 2.3. **Percentage of Students in Grades 6-12 Who Have Been Suspended or Expelled, By Race, 2007.** *Source:* **U.S. Department of Education, National Center for Education Statistics, Parent and Family Involvement in Education Survey of the National Household Education Surveys Program (NHES), 2007. Asians did not meet reporting standards for expulsion due to small numbers of expelled Asian students.**

There are striking differences among them. Only 11 percent of Asians and 16 percent of whites had been suspended, and only 1 percent of white students had been expelled in 2007. Too few Asians had been expelled to meet reporting standards.

In contrast to whites and Asians, 43 percent of black and 22 percent of Hispanic students had been suspended in 2007. Almost 13 percent of black students had received the stiffest penalty, expulsion, which was more than four times the rate of the next category of students (Hispanics). To the extent that these higher figures represent actual student misbehavior, rather than discriminatory enforcement of discipline, this indicates that especially in schools with large proportions of black students, there is less focus on academic matters than in schools with smaller proportions of these students.

School safety has become an increasingly serious, literally a life or death issue. Figure 2.4 considers percentages of white, black, and Hispanic students in 2011 that felt too unsafe to go to school in the previous year, that were threatened with a weapon, and that were in fights in school. In some respects, Hispanics were the most disadvantaged of the three. Over 9 percent of Hispanics felt that their schools were unsafe places, compared to 7 percent of blacks and fewer than 4 percent of whites.

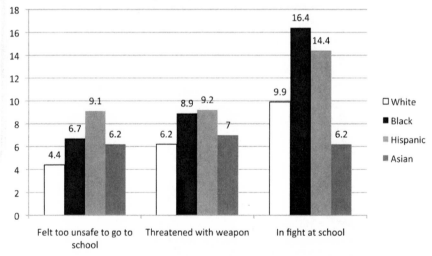

Figure 2.4.   Percentage of Students Reporting Violence on School Grounds, by Race and Hispanic Ethnicity, 2011. *Source*: **U.S. Department of Education, National Center for Education Statistics, Digest of Education Statistics, 2012, Table 194**

Almost one in ten Hispanics and blacks were threatened with a weapon in school, compared to about 6 percent of whites and 7 percent of Asians. If Hispanic and black students are going to schools where about one in ten are threatened with weapons and feel too unsafe to attend, is it hard to understand why other groups, including many Hispanics and blacks themselves, would seek to avoid those schools?

On a somewhat less serious but probably much more common measure of school disorder, black students reported the most problems. One out of every six black students (16.4 percent) reported having been in a fight in the previous year. Hispanics are not too far behind, since 14.4 percent were in fights. By contrast, 10 percent of white students and only 6.2 percent of Asians reported having been in a fight. Thus, it stands to reason that if there are more incidents of problematic behavior among minority students, then schools with large minority populations will have more incidents.

Probably the most routine form of disorder in schools concerns student disrespect toward teachers. Another, gang activity, is more serious. Those who have sufficient resources to do so would clearly want to avoid sending their children to schools with gangs, and would not want their children in schools in which the students were disrespectful and disruptive.

Figure 2.5 shows percentages of middle schools reporting problems with student disrespect for teachers and problems with gang activities by the racial make-up of schools. Among schools with less than 5 minority enrollments, 16 percent reported problems with disrespect toward teachers and only 6 percent reported gang problems. The greater the proportion of minority students, the greater was the probability of disorder on both of these measures. Even more significantly, close to two-thirds of middle schools (61 percent) with mostly minority students reported that they had problems with the indicator of serious disorder, gangs.

Parental involvement and school order contribute substantially to educational value of schools in a marketplace of competing institutions. These are also clearly associated with the racial composition of schools. What, then, does this mean for equality of opportunity in schools? In the following section, we will look carefully at this question in order to consider how school compositions can undermine efforts to create equality of opportunity through redistribution.

WHAT DOES THIS MEAN FOR EQUALITY OF OPPORTUNITY?

The most important investment in education made by any family is the investment of its children. The school that receives a child also receives all the years of socialization and attention that the parents have been able to give him or her. The school receives the parents' own education, knowledge, and attitudes that have been communicated to the child, and which the child then spreads throughout the school in her interactions with students and faculty.

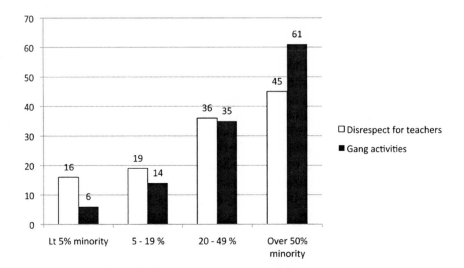

Figure 2.5.   Percentage of Public Middle Schools Reporting Regular Disrespect for Teachers and Gang Activities, by Percentage Minority Enrollment, 2005-06. *Source*: **U.S. Department of Education, National Center for Education Statistics, Crime and Safety Surveys, 2006, Table 10.**

Schools chosen by educationally advantaged parents, who generally also have the economic ability to make choices, have concentrations of the best-prepared students. Since these students make their schools desirable to others, the socioeconomic sorting becomes a trend of exclusivity, with educational elites drawn to schools that contain those like themselves. The inequality of schools is then reinforced by the ongoing actions of parents.

As we have pointed out previously, parental involvement in schooling is closely associated with race and social class, with white parents and middle to upper class parents showing much higher levels of involvement than the parents of black and Hispanic children. To recognize this is not to "blame" minority parents. Their lower involvement may well be the consequence of more limited time and lack of familiarity with the educational system. In any event, acknowledging a documented fact, as uncomfortable as it is, is not the same as making a moral judgment.

Parental involvement contributes to the quality of a school in many ways that are not strictly financial in character. It is also a major source of the financial resources of schools. As one work on educational economy pointed out, parent-teacher organizations "raise significant funds in a variety of ways: product sales, auctions, competitions, galas, and other fundraising drives. Traditional product fundraising generates an average of $13,000 per school. Nationwide, almost $2 billion is raised each school year by parent and teacher organizations."[17]

In the hyper-competitive educational environment of Manhattan, parent groups at the most sought-after public schools (also termed "public-private" schools, for good reason) raise upwards of one million dollars or more per year to supplement the public funding provided by the city.[18] This money is used to do everything from paying for field trips, buy iPads, hire full-time enrichment teachers, and even hire fitness coaches for recess and full-time chefs to assist the chef already paid for by the Education Department.

The city is aware of the big disparities between these affluent schools and the many high poverty, high minority public schools that typify New York City. It has therefore tried to equalize these gross differences by working with nonprofit groups to support low-income schools. But the best the city could do is contribute an additional $216 per high-needs student beyond what was already budgeted by the Education Department, compared to one high-rolling PTA that spends more than $1,600 per student.[19]

In addition to fundraising, parental volunteer work makes a difference in the value of schools. "Nationally one survey estimated that almost 3.4 million public school volunteers logged approximately 109 million work hours in 2000. This was reported to be roughly equivalent to 52,000 full-time staff."[20]

Schools that offer good educations by providing students with well-prepared, reasonably motivated schoolmates, then, also end up having an edge in the availability of parental labor and in the financing produced by parents. While the amount that resources can contribute to school quality is a point of debate, few researchers would argue that parental involvement in schools is unimportant. Schools become a way that middle class parents can help to find places for their children in the middle-class:

> Schools in socio-economically middle and upper class neighborhoods thus receive more resources than schools in disadvantaged neighborhoods: the latter typically lack volunteers or as many volunteers as the former. This could be regarded as exacerbating equity problems, which would not necessarily be resolved by the presence of parent volunteers in the schools without them. After all, differences in the quality of volunteer help might still leave us with an inequity.[21]

Few parents will engage in active fundraising, or will volunteer hours of service in schools that do not serve their own children. To do so would be to take scarce time away from their own offspring. Similarly, every dollar that a family gives to a school its own children do not attend is a dollar that the family cannot give to the school that its children do attend.

When asked if they'd consider pooling their money with other schools, the co-president of a big spending PTA in Manhattan that raised over $1 million in the 2009–2010 school year answered demurely, "I think it's very hard to raise money and not have control over how that money is spent."[22] In short, parents not only tend to give time and money directly to the schools that educate their children, but they support property taxes when their children are in the schools that receive the benefits of those taxes.

When parents choose to place their children in private schools, they remove their own participation, as well as the academic skills of their children, from public schools.[23] Moreover, they give themselves an incentive to be reluctant to raise property taxes for public schools. While they may agree with the proposition that all children have the right to an equal education, placing higher taxes on top of their tuition payments takes funds away from their children.

Moving into public school districts where there are few economically disadvantaged children is in the best interest of their own children. However, this also deprives the districts where disadvantaged minorities are concentrated of middle class economic and social resources. Since property values tend to rise with high test scores, as noted earlier, they also tend to fall with low test scores.

Therefore, the racial test score gap means that the concentration of white families outside of minority areas hits those areas twice. It removes higher scoring students, making test scores go down, driving property values and potential tax revenues down. The absence of white families also means that many who have the revenues to pay property taxes are lost to minority school districts.

Elite programs or rigorous tracking within schools constitute the third primary alternative for those seeking the best opportunities for their children. This alternative is in many ways preferable to the other two. In particular, it contributes more than the other alternatives to maximizing the opportunities of the disadvantaged.

Advanced placement tracks and gifted classes can provide pay-offs to those in them, while helping to ensure that the schools that contain them receive the tax support and involvement of historically advantaged groups. These kinds of within-school stratification do not promote equality of opportunity, though. By definition, those in the non-elite tracks will enjoy fewer opportunities than those in the elite tracks.

Our economic model suggests that when people are prevented from seeking the self-interest of their children in one way, this simply pushes them toward other alternatives. If, for example, students are re-distributed throughout a school district, the general level of school quality will go down. The quality of special advanced placement tracks may go up, though, as educationally advantaged parents desperately seek to have their children enter these tracks.

While some parents seek special slots inside of districts trying to redistribute educational opportunity, other parents of relatively high performing groups will have their children move out to other school districts or to non-public schools. As the proportion of disadvantaged minority students increases with these departures, competition for the few top schools or programs becomes even more intense. Ironically, a school system that in general shows deplorable achievement may end up with small pockets of outstanding performance—like Benjamin Franklin High gifted in the abysmally low-achieving New Orleans school district.

In the following chapter, we will turn to consider brief histories of desegregation in school districts across the United States. We encourage readers to keep our sketch of the economy of educational opportunity in mind and to think about whether this sketch does seem to describe the patterns of occurrences in those districts. Before we look at these districts, though, it might be worthwhile to mention the implications of our model for school vouchers and for other twenty-first-century efforts to move children from low-performing to high-performing schools.

As we will discuss in greater detail in the last chapter, reform efforts including the No Child Left Behind Act of 2001 come out of the history of school desegregation and have a great deal in common with desegregation. Like school desegregation, most voucher programs and related school reforms aim at the redistribution of opportunity. Unlike command and control approaches to school desegregation, these reforms generally emphasize freedom of choice of individual families, an emphasis that appeals to the fundamental political values of many Americans.

Still, our description of the educational marketplace leads us to be skeptical of redistribution in general as a means of truly equalizing educational opportunities. If education is an exclusive good, with a value established by its consumers, then the redistribution of advantaged and disadvantaged students always tends to lower the educational quality enjoyed by the advantaged. If low-performing students in failing public schools are allowed to transfer wholesale to the highest-performing public schools per NCLB guidelines, then academic levels at these receiver schools will necessarily fall by some given amount.

Elite private schools maintain their value by being selective. Even if the state were to subsidize the tuition payments of those who would not otherwise be able to pay, those elite schools would quickly become non-elite if they were to adopt open admissions policies. According to our model, the top-notch students would begin to leave.

If these private institutions continued their selectivity, a few, bright, hardworking minority children would be able to enter with vouchers. While this would be good for the best minority students, it would make little impact on racial and ethnic or socioeconomic inequality of education. With subsidies removing the barriers of paying tuition or a high mortgage, then the best schools would become even more intensely competitive academically.

With the very best students concentrated in the most selective schools, other schools would be left as the default for those who fell behind in the accelerating academic race. The result of rising academic standards would probably be greater educational inequality, not less. In addition, given the continuing achievement gap in race and ethnicity, much of that inequality would be along racial and ethnic lines.

THE SCHOOL MARKETPLACE IN PRACTICE

Because schools are markets of exclusivity, the value of an education is largely established by the students in the classrooms on the basis of the assets they bring with them from their families and communities. Unfortunately, the long history of racial and ethnic inequality in the United States means that black, Hispanic, Asian, and white pupils, on average, bring different and unequal assets to the classroom. Therefore, faced with governmental attempts to redistribute educational opportunities by redistributing public school students, families who want to hang on to their advantages will attempt to turn to one of the four following strategies.

If there are other public school systems available, parents may move or even falsify an address so that they can go to a market that offers a higher quality product. If there are private schools, or if they can create private schools, they may leave the public system altogether. If there are good educational stores inside of generally worsening markets, they will go to the good internal stores. In other words, if middle-class families can concentrate their children in magnet schools or gifted programs, they may seek the internal option.

Finally, as a fourth option, if none of the above alternatives is affordable, available, or palatable, parents who are able to do so may arrange to opt out of formal schooling altogether. They may pull their children from an untenable educational situation and turn to homeschooling.

Each of these strategies is, of course, a form of racial and economic segregation, undercutting governmental efforts to control the market through desegregation efforts. Which strategy a family takes depends on which alternative is the most readily available, given the family's abilities to bear the costs. A low-income family, whether black, Hispanic, or white, may want to get out of an impoverished inner-city public school, but not have the means to do so. Middle-class families, disproportionately white in our nation, have more options available to them.

The most common choice is probably to avoid schools that are redistributing students—the classic white flight. If there are no other desirable school districts in a desegregating area and a family with choices must live there, though, then private schools may be desirable. Private schools can be costly, however, so magnet programs, offering a kind of private school experience inside of public schools, may be a family's best choice. Though still the least chosen option of the four, an increasing number of Americans are simply opting out of formal schooling altogether.

These different strategies suggest that governmental attempts to restructure the educational economy simply will not work. Education can never be a true monopoly. Racial and economic segregation, as an expression of white middle-class self-interest, therefore tends to continually subvert such efforts.

At this point, the reader might answer: well, I suppose this gloomy view might make some theoretical sense, but reality is a good deal more complicated than theory. Surely there is a chance that we can create a more just and equitable society through our schools? Our answer is to look at what has actually happened in American schools over the history of desegregation and see if the patterns of events have matched our picture of the struggle to redistribute students as a radical, self-defeating process.

Too many large and small school districts have been subject to federal desegregation efforts for us to look at every one. We have chosen a broad selection of locations—some notorious, some less so—to examine similarities and differences. We do believe that our examples are representative of the histories of other places, and we think that people who live in other parts of the country may well see many of the experiences of their own communities reflected here.

In order to show that our account of how educational markets and consumer choices have undermined desegregation across the country, in the following two chapters we will set forth examples of what actually happened in school districts. Choosing a wide sampling of school districts from the northeastern, southern, midwestern, and western parts of the United States, we made no effort to select cases that would support our argument.

Although we have tried to be roughly chronological in following the years desegregation began in different districts, the long duration of cases means that most were going on simultaneously. Some of the districts included in the next two chapters are in large, old industrial cities. Others, such as Dallas and Baton Rouge, are in post-industrial, mostly suburban metropolitan areas. One is struck, though, by an essential sameness that runs throughout. In none of these districts did desegregation really seem to work out as intended.

Despite the general similarity among the districts, we ask the reader to pay attention to some striking patterns. These patterns occurring in history are those that we have argued would result from schools as markets of exclusivity. In a number of the locations, attempts to redistribute students were followed by the near total abandonment of entire districts by whites.

The huge public school system of New York, the nation's largest classic urban area, became an almost entirely minority school district. Even little pockets of white representation such as Rosedale, ironically more racially integrated than the city as a whole, were wiped out. Chicago and Milwaukee, also old industrial centers, became cities in which white students were extremely rare.

Some may argue that whites left New York, Chicago, and Milwaukee public schools for reasons that had nothing to do with the schools, that this was simply a reflection of white abandonment of the cities for the suburbs. Undoubtedly, schools were not the only cause of movement to the suburbs. However, such a defense of coercive desegregation policies would be strange indeed. Essentially, such a defense maintains that the policies would have worked, if only demographic realities had been more cooperative.

The claim that schools had nothing to do with suburbanization rings hollow, though. Repeatedly, parents proclaimed that they were leaving desegregating districts because of their school situations. Later, the same groups of people who said that they were leaving because of desegregation were gone. Surely, one has to consider the possibility that actions had something to do with clearly stated intentions. In addition, the abandonment of desegregating districts was not only a movement from central cities to suburbs. Largely suburban districts, such as Los Angeles, Dallas, and Baton Rouge, also lost their white students.

All of the districts that saw whites moving across district lines had at least one characteristic in common: There were other places to go. In this respect, the urban-suburban question was relevant. Moving out of New York or Chicago, or settling in a suburb upon moving to one of these metropolitan areas, meant that the disproportionately middle-class white families could put their relatively well-prepared children into schools with other children who were academically well-prepared.

Despite some general similarities across districts, there are also differences. Some districts have been heralded as desegregation successes. We have been unable to locate any cases in which desegregation could really be described as a "success," but the outcomes were less disastrous in some places than in others. In some situations, whites and middle-class blacks did remain in school systems. In others, limited inter-district voluntary transfers and other strategies did hold out improved opportunities for some minority students.

Little Rock Central High School, opened to black enrollment before the era of coercive redistribution of students, became a majority black school, but it did retain a substantial white student body. Charlotte, a critical district in the history of coercive desegregation, actually retained a large white proportion even with its busing program. Why, then, wasn't there substantial white flight from these places?

Part of the answer is that there were few more desirable places to go. Charlotte was not surrounded by potentially desirable school districts and it included the school area of Charlotte-Mecklenburg. Districts that did not have competing districts had effective monopolies, in which the educational product could be manipulated and customers would still be likely to consume it.

The success of districts without competitors at retaining students suggests that efforts at metropolitan desegregation were based on a sound approach that would have made good sense to John D. Rockefeller. If there is a challenge to a monopoly, extend the monopoly to include it. The problem with this reasoning is that if the perceived quality of the product goes down enough, the customers who have the mobility and financial resources will travel pretty far for an alternative. In Indianapolis, the historical testimony indicates that whites moved beyond the distant reach of the metropolitan public schools.

A variation on the inter-district approach might be to keep the educational markets essentially segregated by geography, while giving a small number of disadvantaged students access to the better schools. The number has to be kept small, of course, because large influxes of the disadvantaged would change the quality of education in the better schools.

Finding ways to move small numbers of disadvantaged students across district boundaries was essentially the kind of metropolitan strategy employed by the State of Connecticut, St. Louis, and by Wisconsin's Chapter 220. This is good for giving individual black students who want to attend majority white schools the opportunity to do so. But it does nothing to significantly change racial balances or to redesign American society.

Even when a wide geographic area is included in the educational monopoly, this still does not shut down all alternatives to the mixed schools intended by judicial desegregation. Private and parochial schools continue to compete with the public school system. As the value of public school education goes down with redistribution, those who can make the sacrifices become more willing to pay the costs of private education.

The districts we have considered in chapter 3 on clear desegregation failures, generally have very high rates of private school attendance. Parents said that they were moving to private schools in order to avoid desegregation. In the case of Baton Rouge, we have been able to document massive white movement into non-public schools, and indeed the creation of non-public schools, immediately following a judge's order to redistribute students by race.

Both the shift to private schools and the shift to other public districts have clear financial implications for desegregating districts. Those whose children attend non-public schools basically pay for education twice. They pay tuition where their children actually attend and they pay taxes for the public schools their children do not attend.

It is not surprising that areas with high private school enrollments frequently have difficulty raising taxes for school spending. This makes the problem of inequality in school funding even greater. School districts that already have poor schools because they enroll students with limited preparation for schooling are further penalized by restricted funding.

Parents in one district are generally reluctant to have their money shifted to another district. Sermons about the duty to treat all young people equally may induce guilt. But they will rarely succeed in getting people to agree to spend less of their money on the preparation of their own children and more of their money on schools their children cannot attend.

Finally, moving from one public school district to another and enrolling in private schools do not exhaust all of the options. The value of an education is established by classmates. Since there is a large and continuing achievement gap between black and white students, under most conditions families likely look for classes composed mainly of whites, although race would certainly be irrelevant in a class that contained top-notch students from all racial groups.

When de facto segregation between schools is reduced by redistributing students, then segregation within schools tends to be one of the results. Magnet programs, gifted and talented programs, and other kinds of elite public school education are often criticized as providing private schools inside of public schools. But if those kinds of special offerings were not available, the students in them would not remain in supposedly desegregated public school systems.

In addition, magnet and related programs must be elite in character. They must be restricted to those with high levels of academic achievement in order to attract and hold the best students. If they just offer unusual and interesting areas of instruction without a selection mechanism in place (such as a test score) then they will attract a wider range of students and the educational quality will go down.

Magnets that are filled through test scores tend to be mainly white (or Asian), as a result of the test score gap. Thus, Little Rock's Central High, a shrine to the history of school integration, still has segregated classes as a result of tracking. When magnets drop achievement as an entrance requirement and attempt to hold on to white students by guaranteeing them places through quotas, this creates new problems.

A supposed tool for desegregation becomes a means of intentionally giving whites access to special resources, while systematically denying equal treatment to blacks. Since the quality of the programs is not maintained by restricting entry to the highly qualified, whites can frequently find better educational products elsewhere. As in Prince George's County, school systems end up keeping black students out of magnet classrooms in order to hold open places to attract white students who are not coming.

Behind the stories of districts that we tell in the next two chapters, we can see families making choices about educational products. The value of these products is largely established by exclusivity. If they can, members of a middle-class family will move into a neighborhood with a highly reputed public school, paying a higher mortgage than they may pay elsewhere.

The school is good because it is attended by children from their own neighborhood. Most of these children have relatively good preparation and come from families who are actively seeking educational advantages. To say that it is a "good school," moreover, is to say that it is better than others, since good is a relative quality and schools are necessarily in competition, if they are not to sink into a general mediocrity.

When a judge or other authority begins to redistribute the advantages and disadvantages of schools, by redistributing students, the good school is no longer so desirable. The family begins to look for other ways to give children an education that will prepare them for a highly and increasingly competitive society. As in Beaumont or Baton Rouge, the family may put its home up for sale and move where there is no forced redistribution.

The family may also do a "virtual" move, entering an educational black market by seeking a false address for school enrollment. Or, it may leave the public system altogether and go to the private sector, where the costs may be greater, but where there is no pretense of equality. Or, instead of moving segregation upward by abandoning a public school district, families may move segregation downward, by demanding tracking and honors classes in order to retain its competitive advantages while participating in the illusion of redistribution.

CHAPTER SUMMARY

In this chapter, we have developed the concept of schools as markets by looking closely at the nature of the educational marketplace. We have investigated the problem of redistributing educational opportunity by thinking more generally about the problems of redistributing resources through controlled markets. The biggest problem is that public schools are never really monopolies. They compete with private schools, with public schools in other districts, and even with homeschooling. When attempts to redistribute educational resources lower the value of those resources, this creates incentives to leave a redistributing school system.

Consistent with the market of exclusivity argument, we have seen that the racial and socioeconomic compositions of schools are related to academic environments. If a family seeks a school with high parental involvement and social order in schools, it will, unfortunately but unavoidably, look for a school with relatively low enrollments of academically disadvantaged minority students. Trying to redistribute students in order to achieve equal opportunity across population groups, then, encourages those who can make choices to examine their options.

We have discussed how this educational marketplace works in practice by providing an overview of pressures and responses in some of the districts that we will discuss in the next two chapters. We will follow this by providing fairly detailed case studies of districts in which attempts to treat schools as monopolies in which students could be redistributed at will resulted in flight across district lines, movement to private schools, and even the secession of suburban neighborhoods from their districts. Following that, we will look at how market choices undermined true desegregation even in some of the districts in which desegregation efforts did not end in utter fiascos.

Chapter Three

Command and Control Failures

Cases of Self-Defeating Policies

So far, we have described schools as markets of exclusivity. The value of an education, we have argued, depends heavily on the clientele of schools. Those who have economic and social resources can create high-performing schools. Those who have these resources also have the capacity to avoid low-performing schools. Unfortunately, social as well as financial resources in the United States are associated with race and ethnicity. This means that attempts to redistribute students by race and ethnicity means not only redistributing advantages, but disadvantages as well.

In the following case histories, we will see how the command and control approach to redistributing students has often resulted in intense de facto segregation in many school districts around the nation. We will also see that the failure of school desegregation across these cases cannot be attributed to a failure of will to enforce, but to the dynamics of the educational marketplace.

BATON ROUGE, LOUISIANA [1]

By the time it ended in 2003, the case of *Davis et al. v. East Baton Rouge Parish School Board* was said to have been the longest running desegregation suit in the nation. It began in 1956, when black parents sued the school board for running a dual school system. During the 1960s, the school board attempted to answer the suit by adopting a "freedom of choice" approach to integrating schools, allowing black and white students to attend schools without regard to race. This resulted in little change in the racial identifications of schools, though, and educational institutions in Louisiana's capital remained distinctly black and white.

Despite the long existence of the East Baton Rouge (EBR) suit, active, court-ordered desegregation in the district only began in 1981. In that year, Federal District Judge John Parker decided that the school board had been running a dual school system for the previous twenty years. Judge Parker therefore ordered the closing of fifteen schools, and developed pairs or clusters of previously black and white schools that were to exchange students through busing in order to achieve racial balances similar to those of the district-wide demographics.

The response to the 1981 decision was immediate. White families said that they would leave the public schools if it were put into effect. The president of the parent-teacher organization at a majority white school, whose daughter was to be transferred to a majority black school in a lower-income neighborhood, declared, "She will not do that. Private schools are starting up every day."[2] Events showed that these were not idle threats.

In the first year of court-ordered busing alone, the East Baton Rouge public school system lost 7,000 white students. Private school waiting lists grew long and new schools started up almost daily. The percentage of white students in the East Baton Rouge school district who attended non-public schools had been going down from 1965 until 1980, from just under a fourth of white students to well under 20 percent just before the judge's decree. From the early 1980s onward, though, this proportion went steadily upward, so that nearly half of the white students in the district were in non-public schools by 2000.

In addition to moving from public to private schools, Baton Rouge area white families also either moved out of the East Baton Rouge school district, or, if they were new arrivals, they settled outside of the school district. Settlement in the adjoining Livingston and Ascension Parishes[3] had been growing slowly before the 1981 decision, but the proportion of the area's white population in these nearby areas began to shoot up rapidly just after the decision.

About one-fourth of the region's white public school students were enrolled outside of the East Baton Rouge district in 1965. By the end of the 1970s, still only about one-third of these white public school students were in adjoining districts. In the two decades after Judge Parker's 1981 ruling though, the proportion of white public school students in the Capital City metropolitan area that were enrolled in the Ascension or Livingston districts grew to about two-thirds.

A longtime school official in one of the districts outside of Baton Rouge told us that the growth of the district's population was "almost exclusively driven by white flight and the initial location of new hires for industry in East Baton Rouge who will not live where they work."[4] Readers should note that this was not a matter of whites leaving some blighted central city for the green lawns of the suburbs. Baton Rouge itself consists almost entirely of suburbs, so that this was movement from the suburbs to the suburbs.

Baton Rouge's loss of white students briefly slowed in the late 1980s. A school system central office administrator with whom we spoke attributed this to a brief experiment with "controlled choice."[5] This was explicitly intended to restore the confidence of those who had lost faith in the local public school system. It relied on magnet programs and special curricula. The experiment broke down, though, because of shortages in funding and difficulties in maintaining support from school officials.

By 1996, East Baton Rouge had changed from a majority white to a majority black district. Two-thirds of the public school students in the district were black, although the proportion had been roughly constant at about 40 percent from 1965 until just before the 1981 court order. Largely to stabilize this chaotic, rapidly changing system, the school board and plaintiffs to the Davis case, including the NAACP, reached a court-approved consent decree in 1996.

The consent decree largely ended busing, and sought, instead, to pump large infusions of funds into the school system, including generous "equity accounts" for historically black schools. The $2.2 billion program hit a speed bump when it went before taxpayers, though, since voters resoundingly defeated a tax and bond proposal to raise money for continued desegregation efforts. With much of the middle class now out of the local public schools, members of the middle class had little interest in taxing themselves for a system many had fled.

Racial differences in school performance fed desires by whites to leave the East Baton Rouge public school system. On the math portion of the 1999 Louisiana Graduation Exit Examination, for example, white students in EBR's public schools answered an average of 72 percent of the questions correctly. Black EBR students answered an average of less than 55 percent of these questions correctly.

Among schools, the very few that ranked in the state's top categories as "School of Academic Excellence" or "School of Academic Distinction" on the 1999 Louisiana Educational Assessment Program tended to be precisely the schools where the remaining white students were still clustered. The one school in the top category was about 80 percent white and the four schools in the next highest category averaged about 55 percent white. At the other end, the forty-six schools in the next to lowest "Academically Below Average" category averaged 87 percent black, and the three "Academically Unacceptable" schools averaged 94 percent black.

As whites continued to leave the desegregating district, they left the less advantaged black students behind. Deputy School Superintendent Clayton Wilcox observed that, "the school system is getting blacker."[6] By the

2002–2003 school year, 73 percent of the public school students in the district were black, and the proportion was a good deal higher in the elementary grades.[7] Several years later, in 2009–2010, 82 percent of the district's students were black. A little under 12 percent were white and the rest were Asian or Hispanic. Most of the white students left in East Baton Rouge in 2010 were in non-public schools (59 percent).[8]

In the mid-2000s, East Baton Rouge schools, like schools in Orleans and some other Louisiana districts, began to turn in desperation to a form of official segregation by school performance within the district. In 2003, alarmed by the low level of school achievement in several districts, the Louisiana legislature passed an act to create the Recovery School District (RSD), a special statewide district that would take over consistently failing schools, as measured by student performance scores.

Although the RSD was most active in Orleans Parish following Hurricane Katrina in 2005, the statewide district also took over the lowest-performing schools in East Baton Rouge, either as schools directly run by the RSD or as charter schools under RSD authority (a common strategy, following the failure of desegregation to resolve the problems of minority students, as we will argue in chapter 5). By fall 2013, eight Baton Rouge schools were listed under RSD direction.[9]

Thus, Baton Rouge had essentially segregated its worst schools from the rest of the district. These schools were also invariably minority concentration schools. For example, the Baton Rouge RSD's Capitol High School, which received a grade of "F" on the 2011–2012 school report card, had only African American students.[10]

Crestworth Learning Academy, also a Baton Rouge RSD middle school, had only African American and only low-income students. It received an "F" on the 2010–2011 school performance score, the most recently available on the school's profile sheet.[11] Dalton Elementary School was 100 percent African American, 100 percent low-income. It also received a score of "F" on the 2010–2011 school performance score.[12]

The RSD may have been a reasonable educational strategy. Desegregation had become impossible. The worst schools were so bad that desperate measures were justified. However the RSD also created a separate internal district of entirely black, entirely poor students within a district of almost entirely black, almost entirely poor students.

Middle-class families with children, both black and white, had already moved out of the core areas of Baton Rouge to the suburbs by the time the Recovery School District came into existence. Concern about the decline of East Baton Rouge schools led to repeated efforts by suburban neighborhoods within the EBR district to break away and form their own systems. The majority black town of Baker became the first to secede in 1999, but Baker contained mostly minority students and saw no improvement in its school system.

Consistent with our argument that being in schools that concentrate advantages pays off, predominantly white breakaway districts had much more success. The Zachary Community School District came into existence in 2003, after residents convinced the state legislature to carve out a new district. By 2011, the Zachary district was Louisiana's top performing district, as measured by the District Performance Score.[13] When the 2013 school results came out in October 2013, the *Times Picayune* newspaper reported that "The Zachary school system north of Baton Rouge maintained its status as the top-rated school system."[14]

In 2005, the citizens of the Central area voted to incorporate as the City of Central, apparently in order to create a separate school system, which was established in 2007. Central also showed a record of achievement much higher than that of East Baton Rouge, and by 2012 the Central school district was the fourth top ranked system in the state.[15]

Like Zachary, Central was among the 12 percent of Louisiana school systems that received an "A" in the 2013 school results.[16] Residents in the southeast part of EBR mounted an effort to follow the examples of Zachary and Central. Frustrated in their attempts to create a separate school system within Baton Rouge, in 2013 the southeast Baton Rouge organization Local Schools for Local Children began calling for a petition to create a new city.[17]

Economists at Louisiana State University estimated that the loss of this middle class, mainly white area, would take $53 million away from the general fund of the rest of the parish. They predicted that the income loss would lead to an increase in taxes in the left over portions. Even with tax increases, the secession of Central would likely result in cuts to police and fire services.[18]

The *Times-Picayune* newspaper gave some insight into the motivations of those calling for the new city of St. George in southeast Baton Rouge. Describing one of the core groups of organizers behind the St. George effort, the newspaper wrote:

> Norman Browning wants out. He wants out of a school district where students bring guns to school, where cell-phone videos capture fistfights, where two teenagers recently knocked out a bus driver's teeth, where a middle schooler set a substitute teacher on fire. He wants out of a school district that is attempting—and, he believes, failing—to cater to 42,000 children, the majority of whom are impoverished and struggling in school.[19]

Critics of this newest effort to split off from East Baton Rouge to get away from the district's school system accused the new city advocates of disingenuously denying the role of race in their desire to leave, and of taking their economic and social resources and leaving low-income, minority students behind. But even if one attributes all of the problems plaguing East Baton Rouge's district to a history of racial oppression, no parent would want to make penance for the sins of ancestors with the sacrifice of his or her own children to a well-documented climate of violence and failure.

CHICAGO, ILLINOIS

Like so many other desegregation cases, the roots of Chicago's lie in the era of the Civil Rights Movement. Several Chicago parents filed suit in 1961, claiming that the city's schools were segregated by race. Two years later, attempting to avoid court action, the school board responded by appointing a panel of experts to study the situation, although the board did not act on the panel's recommendations.

The situation turned more serious in 1965, when the U.S. Commission of Education froze federal funds to the city because of the continuing racial identification of the schools. Political connections temporarily rescued the city, though, because Mayor Richard J. Daley contacted President Lyndon Johnson, and Johnson rescinded the Commission's cutoff. For the following decade, Chicago largely avoided student redistribution.

Chicago School Superintendent James F. Redmond made some efforts at desegregation, proposing the development of magnet schools and the use of busing in 1967. Still, these types of programs made little headway for the next decade. A new era of pressure from above began in March 1976, when the Illinois State Board of Education told the Chicago Board of Education that the city was not complying with the state's desegregation rules, and that the state would shut off all funds.

The city board responded to the state's complaint by initiating its "Access to Excellence" strategy. Chicago school officials pitched "Access to Excellence" as a way of relieving overcrowding in the primarily black schools in its central area. Overcrowding was indeed a problem in many of the central city schools. Clearly, though, much of the motivation for the strategy was the retention of state funds and avoidance of a federal lawsuit.

This 1977 plan aimed at the voluntary transfer of 6,573 black students in fifteen overly crowded schools to fifty-one schools in Chicago's nearly all-white sections. Some would be transported by school bus and some would be given tokens to ride public transportation to their new schools. By the beginning of the 1977 school year, though, only 1,000 black students had chosen to participate in the program, reportedly because of threats of white violence.[20]

The U.S. Supreme Court added to the complications of desegregation in Chicago, and elsewhere in the nation. The Court ruled at the beginning of 1977 that the affluent, all-white Chicago suburb of Arlington Heights could enact zoning restrictions that would prevent the building of racially integrated housing for people with moderate and low incomes. To be unconstitutional, the zoning would have had to be clearly racially discriminatory in intent, and not just consequence.[21]

This had two important implications for desegregation. First, it raised the requirements for demonstrating discrimination, in both schools and neighborhoods. Second, it meant that high-income neighborhoods could legally keep out lower-income people, making it more difficult to integrate schools by integrating neighborhoods. Exclusive neighborhoods conflicted with goals for achieving inclusive schools.

The voluntary busing may have been voluntary on the part of those riding the school buses and public transport out of central city locations. It was far from voluntary from the perspective of those in the suburbs who were receiving the transfers. The controversy turned violent on September 11, 1977, when whites from Chicago's Southwest Side area held a candlelight vigil in protest, and an angry black counter-protestor drove a car into the crowd.[22] White mothers picketed the schools that were receiving central city students, and as many as five hundred white students staged a walkout.[23]

Just two years after the voluntary desegregation program began in Chicago, a report to the State Superintendent of Education concluded that the $35 million program had had virtually no impact on desegregating the city's schools. According to the report, 90.3 percent of black students in Chicago would have to be re-assigned to white schools in order to accomplish desegregation.[24] Allowing choice would not achieve the desired goals, even if only the families of minority students could choose.

By October 1979, based on a two-year investigation by the Department of Health, Education and Welfare's Office of Civil Rights, the federal government accused Chicago of maintaining segregated schools. The federal government demanded that local school officials come up with a plan for redistributing the system's 475,000 students, who were at that time 60 percent black, 22 percent white, 15 percent Hispanic, and 2 percent Asian. The Board of Education rejected the HEW conditions, laying itself open to the lawsuit it had tried to avoid.[25]

For the next year, Chicago and the federal government negotiated. Finally, on September 24, 1980, the Chicago Board of Education, the U.S. Justice Department, and U.S. District Judge Milton I. Shadur came to an agreement on citywide desegregation. The agreement established a broad framework for action, but no specific quotas or numbers of students at particular schools. Acknowledging that demographics dictated that many students would remain in segregated schools, the agreement established that students in majority black or Hispanic schools would be given compensatory education programs.

While majority black or Hispanic schools were acceptable, though, majority white schools were another matter. According to Drew S. Days III,

Assistant U.S. Attorney for Civil Rights, "the board would have a very heavy burden to justify majority white schools."[26] From the point of view of numbers, the reluctance to allow majority white schools made sense. Whites, after all, had gone down to under 19 percent of the school population by the beginning of the 1980 school year.

As white students dwindled in numbers, though, increasingly the options open to white families were to place their children in minority-dominated, often low-income schools, or escape from the Chicago system. Given the reluctance of white parents to place their children in schools in which their own racial group was in the minority, this essentially guaranteed that white flight, a fact of life in Chicago for decades, would take on an added speed and volume.

The Board of Education passed a new desegregation measure in the spring of 1981, delaying busing until 1983, and limiting white enrollment to 70 percent of any school. Under this measure, schools with too many white students would have to gradually cut down on their white enrollments. Those who did not succeed in getting rid of white students would have special programs imposed on them, such as receiving forced transfers.[27]

Although white avoidance of majority black schools was certainly not the only reason for white movement out of Chicago, the unwillingness of white families to send their children into schools in which the children would be surrounded by economically disadvantaged minority group members helped to eliminate the remaining white neighborhoods in the city. By the time of the 1980 census, Chicago was "a highly segregated city in which an expanding black ghetto is displacing whites at its leading edge and leaving shattered, abandoned areas in its wake."[28]

The public received a glimpse of a small part of the on-going cost of desegregation in February 1981. At that time, Chicago Board of Education special counsel for school desegregation Robert Howard billed the school board $87,732 for about five months of legal work on the agreement with the federal government.[29] This was not, of course, the final bill, and it in fact represented only a miniscule portion of the total expense of this process.

Represented by Mr. Howard, in 1983, the school board asked Judge Shadur to force the federal government to provide funds for the desegregation agreement the board had made with the government in 1980. Over a two-year period, the Chicago school system had paid $93.6 million in its own money to implement the agreement, and it expected to pay another $67 million in 1983–1984. Since the school board was facing a deficit of $200 million, the members did not know where they would come up with the money.[30]

Chicago had difficulty getting money out of a federal government that had imposed an expensive line of action on the city. After Judge Shadur ordered Washington, D.C. to pay for part of Chicago's school desegregation efforts, the U.S. Department of Education responded that it did not have the funds and the Justice Department appealed the order. Illinois Democratic Representative Sidney Yates tried to step in by introducing a bill in Congress to give Chicago $20 million.

After the bill passed, though, President Ronald Reagan vetoed it, saying that Judge Shadur had violated the principle of separation of the powers of the judiciary and legislature by freezing other forms of federal spending in Chicago until Washington supplied money for the Board of Education.[31] After the 7th Circuit U.S. Court of Appeals upheld Judge Shadur's order, in September 1983, Chicago did get its $20 million, but this was less than a fourth of what the Board of Education was by then actually spending on desegregation efforts.[32]

Eventually, even the federal judiciary came to recognize that it was not possible to redistribute white students a district does not have. U.S. District Judge Charles P. Kocoras declared at the beginning of 2003 that the agreement between the federal government and the district of the 1980s was no longer workable. He ordered the district to come up with a new desegregation plan, which was approved by the court in the spring of 2004. The only integration possible in Chicago schools in 2004 involved mixing black and Hispanic students. By this time the city's public school students were 51 percent black, 36 percent Hispanic, 9 percent white, and 3 percent Asian.[33]

After decades of expensive and contentious efforts to shift students around, the futility of desegregation had become evident. Judge Kocoras finally lifted Chicago's consent decree in September 2009. Chicago Public school officials had urged this step, "saying it would free up money spent on transportation and other services needed to comply with the decree. Further, they noted that, with just 9 percent white enrollment, more integration was impossible."[34]

At the hearing on the decree, "more than a dozen Chicago public school students testified . . . that a 28-year old desegregation decree has failed them," reported the *Chicago Sun-Times.* "They begged for more diversity, more and better books, and better teachers in those schools CPS said it has been unable to desegregate—all of which the 1980 decree was supposed to address."[35] The pleas for more and better books and perhaps also better teachers were understandable. But the school system obviously had no way of furnishing more diversity.

Following the end of the consent decree, the Hispanic proportion continued to increase, becoming a plurality of Chicago students (44.1 percent) by the 2011–2012 school year. Because of this growth in Hispanic representation, black students were no longer the majority, making up 41.6 percent of Chicago students in 2011–2012. Whites, however, were still a small minority, at only 8.8 percent of students, and were concentrated in the system's magnet and selective schools. Nearly nine out of ten Chicago public school students were classified as low-income by 2012.[36]

The federal government forced Chicago to spend millions of dollars on programs that had no discernible positive impact. Although the white proportion of the student population probably would have declined even without desegregation, active efforts to make white students into a minority in any schools they would attend virtually guaranteed their departure. Most remarkable of all, the mostly black and Hispanic leaders of the school district still had to negotiate "desegregation plans" with the federal government until Judge Kocoras agreed to end oversight on the urging of the mostly minority administrators of Chicago's schools.

Desegregation efforts did not accomplish any narrowing of racial differences in school performance. Journalist Steve Bogira, in June 2013, cited a University of Chicago study that found that between 1990 and 2009 (while Chicago was still under its consent decree) "racial gaps in achievement steadily increased. White students made more progress than Latino students, African-American students fell further behind all other groups. White, Asian, and Latino students improved modestly in reading, but there were 'virtually no improvements' among African-American students, at the elementary or high school levels."[37]

DALLAS, TEXAS

The process of desegregation began in Dallas in 1960, when United States District Judge Thomas W. Davidson ordered the integration of Dallas schools in *Borders v. Rippy*. Little happened until a black man brought suit against the city district in 1970 because his son was not allowed to attend an all-white school in his neighborhood.[38] The court order that was consequently issued in 1971, and which in part mandated ending the racial achievement gap, was appealed.

In July 1975, the United States Court of Appeals for the Fifth Circuit ruled that Dallas put a desegregation plan into effect by the start of the second semester of the 1975–1976 school year. The following year, in April, a federal judge handed down an order calling for the division of the Dallas Independent School District into six sub-districts and for busing 17,328 of the district's 141,000 students. The bused students were to come from all racial groups.

Among the students to be bused under the 1975 plan, 51 percent would be black, 38 percent would be white, and 11 percent would be Hispanic. School officials at the time estimated that the busing plan would cost $26.3 million. At the beginning of the active shuffling of students around Dallas based on race, there were almost equal numbers of black and white students, since 44 percent of the district's pupils were black, 41 percent were white, and 13 percent were Latino.[39]

After two decades of court control, Dallas finally managed to obtain unitary status on July 26, 1994. In the order granting this status, the court criticized the school system for its apparent reluctance to put desegregation practices into effect over the years. As a condition for unitary status, the court required Dallas schools to maintain programs such as Majority to Minority transfers, and to continue other desegregation strategies.

The school system responded by establishing a Desegregation Monitoring division in its Department of Evaluation, Accountability and Information Systems. By the school year 2000–2001, the Desegregation Monitoring Division had a budget of $561,538,[40] nearly half of which went to the salaries of four employees. The division's assistant superintendent received a salary in 2000 of $91,599,[41] which would equate to $126,457 in 2014.

The Dallas Independent School District was finally released from all court oversight in 2003. The name of the desegregation Monitoring Division was changed to the "Equity and School Choice Department" at this time, but it ostensibly still had the same function,[42] even though Judge Barefoot Sanders, in granting unitary status, decreed that "the segregation prohibited by the United States Constitution, the United States Supreme Court and federal statutes no longer exists in the city district."[43]

Whites within the city of Dallas had largely abandoned the public school system by the time Judge Sanders declared that segregation no longer existed. Over one-third of the non-Hispanic whites in the city were in non-public schools. Although non-Hispanic whites were 62 percent of all public and non-public students in the 2002–2003 school year, only 7 percent of the public schools students were white.

Most Dallas public school students were Latino (59 percent) or black (33 percent) by 2002–2003. Any efforts at desegregation made by the well-paid assistant superintendent for desegregation monitoring, would have necessarily been aimed at putting Latinos and blacks together, because there were too few whites to integrate. Even members of the two minority groups showed a high degree of isolation from each other, though.

A. Maceo Smith High School, for example, was 94 percent black in 2002–2003, and slightly under 6 percent Latino. Lincoln High School was 96 percent black and 3.4 percent Latino. On the other side, Jefferson High School was 87 percent Hispanic and 9.4 percent black, and Moises Molina High was 88 percent Hispanic and 9.1 percent black. The lower grades were even more racially and ethnically segregated than the high schools.

Academic outcomes had certainly not been equalized by three decades of desegregation. Mean SAT scores for the class of 2002 came to only 850 for the Dallas Independent School District, compared to 986 for the state. The low score was chiefly a result of the high percentage of minority students, since black students in the district scored only 790 and Latino students scored 858, compared to 1,057 for white students.

By contrast with the students in the DISD, students in the mostly white nearby Dallas County district of Highland Park averaged 1194 on the SAT. Students in the Irving district, also in the Dallas region, with a somewhat larger minority population than Highland Park, scored 999.[44] Dallas-area school populations had largely sorted themselves out by race and ethnicity since the beginning of desegregation, and the sorting was closely connected to test results.

Given the continuing low performance among minority students and, by definition, schools with large minority student populations, families who were looking for good schools, as indicated by test results, would reasonably avoid schools or school districts with predominantly black or Hispanic students. During the decade following the granting of unitary status, they apparently did just that. By the 2012–2013 school year, only 4.6 percent of DISD students were white, while 69.5 percent were Hispanic and 23.8 percent were black.[45]

Readers should remember that Dallas is a decentralized, suburban, automobile-based city. It is not, like the older cities of the United States, formed around a decaying industrial inner city, home to minority group members who have been left behind as newer suburbs grow in clusters around the center. Dallas does have poor neighborhoods, of course (south Dallas), and the non-poor seek to avoid settling in these neighborhoods, or sending their children to school in them. But we cannot explain the failure of desegregation in Dallas by claiming that it would have worked if only whites had not just happened to move out of central city areas for reasons other than desegregation. As we look at different types of metropolitan areas and school districts, the striking fact is that the judicially mandated redistribution of students did not seem to work well anywhere. When movement to the suburbs was not the dominant response to redistribution of students, other strategies undermined the monopolistic efforts of planners.

BEAUMONT, TEXAS

Two years after desegregation efforts began in Dallas, the legal process started in another Texas district, Beaumont. In 1962, the Reverend Edward Brown filed a suit against the Beaumont school district. The Reverend Brown's son, Edward Brown II, had been denied enrollment at Fletcher Elementary, a school near the Brown home. Texas in the early 1960s was not Arkansas in the late 1950s, though, and the Beaumont Independent School District responded to the lawsuit by announcing in 1963 that it would begin integrating all the schools in the district, one grade each year, beginning with the first grade.

This did not succeed in redistributing the students of Beaumont's racially concentrated schools, though, and the city went through a period of conflict and oversight by the U.S. Department of Justice through the 1960s and early 1970s. According to a civil rights attorney cited by the *Beaumont Enterprise* newspaper, the district was so tense at this time that it seemed always about to break out in violence.[46] In 1975, the district came up with a desegregation plan that the Department of Justice approved. It combined its two major high schools and re-drew the attendance boundaries for all schools.

The wealthier adjacent district of South Park was distinct from Beaumont through those years, but it had its own desegregation struggles. The U.S. Government ordered South Park to desegregate in 1970, and the district drew up new attendance zones. White reaction was almost immediate. Many white families either put their children in private schools or, even more drastically, sold their homes and moved to other counties.

"Within 30 days, the neighborhoods were vacant and virtually every house for sale," said an attorney for the South Park school district.[47] Of the 200 to 300 students assigned to formerly black Hebert High School in 1970, only 100 attended the first day of school and only ten of those remained by the end of the first month.[48] In 1981, U.S. District Judge Robert Parker came up with his unique "ping-pong" desegregation plan for Beaumont. Families of students drew ping-pong balls for assignment to schools, and then the students were bused all over the district.

Two years later, the Beaumont and South Park school districts merged, creating a single large district. In 1994, seeking a way to return to neighborhood schools, members of a biracial coalition of citizens drew up an agreement with the school board that neighborhood schools would be allowed provided all students were guaranteed equal access to superior schools. No one seemed to point out the obvious contradiction between "equality" and "superiority." This ended most of the long-distance busing around the district.

After 1994, though, schools began to re-segregate. By 2003, Beaumont's Central High School was 82 percent black and only 3 percent white, while Ozen High School was 92 percent black and only 2 percent white. The white high school students were heavily concentrated in West Brook, which was 55 percent white and 30 percent black. Several of Beaumont's elementary schools were 100 percent black.

In 2007, after almost four decades under a desegregation order, the school district sought and was granted unitary status by Judge Thad Heartfield of the Eastern District of Texas. By the time desegregation had finally ended, though, the racial redistribution of students had become moot. After decades of busing and the ping-pong plan, there were not enough white students left to accomplish any kind of racial balance.

In reporting the granting of unitary status, the *Beaumont Enterprise* news-paper noted that in the 2006–2007 school year, 51 percent of the district's 9,479 students were black, 37.2 percent were Hispanic, and 7 percent were Asian. Whites were the smallest minority of all, making up only 4.8 percent of the district's public school students.[49] The dearth of white students was not because there were no whites in the geographic area. The population of the city of Beaumont in the 2010 census was 40 percent white, 47 percent black, and 13 percent Hispanic.

Thus, although there were nearly as many white residents as black, whites in the early twenty-first century were not sending children to the district's public schools, either because white families with children were settling elsewhere or because those whites in Beaumont were finding other educa-tional opportunities for their children. At the end of decades of expensive desegregation, the schools had very few white students left.

LOS ANGELES, CALIFORNIA

The desegregation fight in Los Angeles began with the case of *Crawford v. Board of Education* in 1963, when black parents filed a suit on behalf of black and Latino students to enable minority children to attend then all-white schools.[50] The California district's first desegregation trial was held in 1967, when white students were a majority of 55 percent. On February 11, 1970, Superior Court Judge Alfred Gitelson found that the school board had operat-ed a segregated system and he ordered it to take action to desegregate.

The school board appealed Judge Gitelson's decision. In March 1975, the court of appeal found in favor of the board. In turn, though, this finding was appealed by the American Civil Liberties Union. At the end of June 1976, the California Supreme Court upheld the 1970 ruling by Judge Gitelson. While the state high court reversed a part of Judge Gitelson's ruling that defined desegregation in terms of specific percentages of students, it ordered the school board to alleviate all of the effects of segregation, regardless of the cause of segregation, and show progress toward that end.

During 1977, the L.A. school board submitted a desegregation plan to the California Supreme Court and began hearings on the plan. In February 1978, Judge Paul Egly issued an order approving the board's plan as a first step toward desegregation. The following year, Egly ordered that mandatory reas-signments of students from current to new schools cover grades one through nine by September 1980, and then include all other grades by 1983.

Judge Egly's order was complicated by many of the characteristics of Los Angeles. It is a huge district, covering 700 square miles, with minority stu-dents most heavily concentrated in South Central L.A. This meant that ex-tremely long daily bus rides would be required to redistribute the city's students. Many of the districts where the white students lived were surrounded by other suburban school districts, making white movement to less threatened school environments relatively easy.

Los Angeles was a harbinger of the future in many other metropolitan areas because its ethnic composition was far more complex than a simple division between black and white. Some of these other ethnic groups, such as Mexican Americans, felt that the desegregation program was not in their own interests.[51] The Los Angeles plan did not appear to take any of these complications into consideration. It was an abstract blueprint imposed from above by command and control planners.

Spurred largely by events in Los Angeles, California voters approved Proposition 1 in 1979, amending the state constitution to prohibit any more busing or school transfers than required under the U.S. Constitution. Although this ended mandatory busing in Los Angeles in 1981 after the Court of Appeals upheld the proposition, voluntary busing of students for school desegregation did continue under a plan approved by Judge Robert B. Lopez in September 1981.

In accordance with the voluntary plan, the school system bused 57,000 voluntary school transferees in 1985. The local NAACP criticized the program in that year, though, because almost all of those being bused were black students. The civil rights organization maintained that a serious attempt to desegregate Los Angeles schools would require busing white students into South Central L.A. Interestingly, Latino education leaders opposed busing, instead favoring greater spending on neighborhood schools within Latino areas.[52]

Los Angeles also tried to desegregate through the common strategy of magnet schools, offering special educational programs in the hopes of appealing to members of all racial groups. The magnet schools tried to maintain enrollments that were 40 percent white and 60 percent nonwhite. By the early 1980s, though, they were already finding it difficult to meet the 40 percent target for white students.[53]

In 1982, as many as ten of the district's eighty-four magnet schools contained no white students at all and eighteen had fewer than 20 percent white students. Only thirty-three were at approximately the target enrollments.[54] Many of the magnet schools were also not providing students with the quality of education promised, and they provided educations that were expensive for taxpayers, but failed to achieve "either distinction or integration."[55]

Meanwhile, faced with declining social environments in low-income, majority black schools, many concerned black parents began behaving exactly like middle-class whites and engaging in various forms of "black flight." "Some . . . are manipulating the school system to their children's advantage [by using false addresses to enroll their children in other school districts].

Others are busing their children to schools in white neighborhoods, placing them in special programs, or leaving the public school system altogether. [56]

Fight over judicial control of the schools continued, even after the Supreme Court upheld Proposition 1. In 1985, voters in West San Fernando Valley, the heart of opposition to busing, elected busing critic and academic David Armor to the Los Angeles School Board out of fear that the area would return to a mandatory program of transporting students around the area. [57]

Trying to maintain elusive racial balances became increasingly difficult as the population of Los Angeles changed over the course of the 1980s. In 1987, with numbers of minority students in the district rapidly increasing, the school board voted to increase minority enrollments to 70 percent at forty-eight magnet schools, while still designating the schools as "integrated." [58] The changing of ratios was controversial.

Some critics accused the school board of intentionally creating segregated schools. Others, particularly in the Valley, were upset because bringing down the acceptable proportion of white students in magnet schools to 30 percent would lower the number of white students who could get into those schools. School board member Roberta Weintraub, speaking to white parents from the Valley, complained that "I'm really tired of our Valley schools getting shafted. My perception is that we will have a massive pullout of the middle class." [59]

With decreasing opportunities for the white middle class families, many tried devious maneuvers to place their children in desirable school environments. School officials responded with intensified efforts at control. Childcare transfers became a common strategy. District policy permitted parents to transfer their children out of their designated schools if the schools did not provide before or after school childcare or if the parents had arranged for off-campus childcare near another school.

The board found that white parents were using fraudulent childcare claims to transfer their children out of minority dominated schools to predominantly white schools. Thus, in the summer of 1988 the board began to refuse this type of exemption to white students transferring into schools that were 70 percent or more white. [60] In the name of desegregation, which had originally meant allowing minority students to attend white schools, Los Angeles had begun officially approving schools that were mostly black or Latino, while energetically discouraging schools that were mostly white.

By June 1988, the pointlessness of the district's long and expensive desegregation suit had become clear. Judge A. Wallace Tashima granted a conditional dismissal of the case that had begun in 1963, and directed the NAACP and the school district to resolve their differences. According to school district counsel Peter James, the dismissal came from the recognition that little could be done to desegregate a school system that was just 17 percent white.[61] After bitter and difficult negotiations between the two parties, the judge finally dismissed the suit in March 1989, twenty-six years after its beginning.

The white proportion of public schools had dropped still further from the previous year, to less than 16 percent. The *Los Angeles Times* reported that there was a wide and persistent gap in academic achievement between the minority students and the small number of whites who were left. "More than 20 years after the Los Angeles Unified School District began its original busing program to integrate schools, the minority pupils in that program are doing little or no better than the students they leave behind in segregated schools and much worse than their white classmates."[62]

In the years following the end of desegregation, the percentage of black students in the Los Angeles Unified School District did decline, as did numbers of black students. The district registered black enrollments of 82,423 in 2005-2006 (11.4 percent of all students), which declined to 69,143 in 2009–2010 (10.2 percent). This did not represent growing desegregation, in the traditional sense of greater contact between minority students and whites, though. Instead, it reflected the demographic changes we discussed above.

Los Angeles schools had become a concentration of Hispanics, who made up about three-fourths of the district's student body (73.4 percent) in 2009–2010. Within the district, schools were generally racially identifiable, mostly as Hispanic, but in some cases as black. In the 2011–2012 school year, for example, Douglass High School was 92.1 percent black and 7.4 percent Hispanic. It had no recorded white students. Camino Nuevo High School, on the other hand, was 96.6 percent Hispanic and only 0.2 percent black. Camino Nuevo had only four white students in that year.[63]

After all of the expense and all of the conflict over desegregation, Los Angeles still had schools that were almost all black or almost all Hispanic. White students had become a scarce commodity. This was not entirely a result of white flight from the schools. Demographic change from immigration also played a large part. (We discuss the effects of demographic changes on school desegregation efforts in more detail in the companion volume to this book.) But the fact remains that social planners' schemes to redistribute students by race had proved futile in the Los Angeles Unified School District.

PASADENA, CALIFORNIA

Pasadena, in Los Angeles County, but with its own district, was far from the well-televised civil rights fight in the South. Like the Los Angeles district, though, it had its own form of segregation in the 1960s. White and black families lived in different neighborhoods, and residential housing patterns maintained segregated schools. In 1970, Federal District Court Judge Manuel Real ordered Pasadena to desegregate its schools, and to begin transferring students from largely black to largely white institutions.

The white proportion of the population had been declining in Pasadena since just after World War II, but in 1970 it began a precipitous drop. In that first year of desegregation alone, about 3,000 students withdrew from the district.[64] Although there were no all-black or all-white schools after 1970, from 1970 to 1973, percentages of whites in the district fell from 49.6 percent to 43.6 percent in kindergarten through 6th grade, and from 58.2 percent to 50.1 percent in junior and senior high schools.[65]

The desegregation program imposed by Judge Real was so widely hated that it became a major political issue. In March 1973, voters in Pasadena elected an anti-busing majority to the school board by a wide margin. Henry Mareschi, leader of the anti-busing faction, argued that half the decline in whites was due to white flight resulting from busing and that if the situation continued, the school population would be only 10 percent white by 1980.[66]

Though substantial, Mareschi overestimated the white decline. When the court order was finally lifted in 1980, white school enrollment had gone down to 29.1 percent of all students, from 53.7 percent when desegregation began. Not all of this drop in white students can be attributed to desegregation. More minority students, especially Latinos, entered the public school system. Still, it was undeniable that white flight had occurred.

Private school enrollments had grown from 19 percent of Pasadena pupils at the start of the court order, up to 26 percent by its conclusion. White families had also moved into other school districts in order to remove their children from the contentious system. "It was not only white flight, but bright flight," lamented school board member Katie Nack. "We lost some of our best minority students too, because of fear of what might happen and because of relaxation of educational standards."[67]

The events of the 1970s gave the system a reputation as one to avoid, so that middle-class people, whether white or of other ethnic and racial groups, often did not flee the schools so much as they did not enter them at all. The incoming director of Pasadena's testing program, William A. Bibiani, complained that, "when I was looking for a house here, several realtors subtly, or not so subtly, hinted that I ought to consider private schools."[68] Mr. Bibiani rejected the realtors' hints, but many homebuyers without his connection to the public school system would have taken the realtors' suggestions more seriously.

Some busing for purposes of racial re-distribution continued after the end of Pasadena's desegregation court order. School officials also tried to draw school attendance boundaries in order to get the greatest possible mix of white, black, Hispanic, and Asian students. Still, the demographics dictated that many schools would be overwhelmingly composed of one ethnic or racial group.

Declines in the white student population continued into the twenty-first century. By 2002, the 23,000-pupil district was 85 percent minority. The families of the relatively few white students who remained in the public school system managed to place their children in classrooms composed largely of other whites. Del Yarborough, the president of the Pasadena NAACP and a long-time teacher and principal in the schools, observed, "we may have had integration in the schools, but segregated classrooms."[69]

The small number of white students in the Pasadena schools was not only a result of the fact that white families had withdrawn from the area. Those who argued for ending busing in the early twenty-first century maintained that "resegregation is improbable because so many of Pasadena's neighborhoods have become residentially integrated."[70] In reality, racial integration of the schools was impossible with so few whites left in the public school system. The substantial numbers of whites remaining in the area by the early 2000s attended over thirty private schools.

The percentage of white students in Pasadena's public schools appeared to have stabilized at 15 percent, the proportion still present during the 2012–2013 school year. However, black students also made up just over 15 percent in that year. As in Los Angeles and many other school districts, the immigration wave of the late twentieth and early twenty-first centuries had rendered the struggles to desegregate not only futile but irrelevant. Close to two-thirds of the students in Pasadena (60.3 percent) by 2012–2013 were Hispanic.[71]

Black students were, of course, much more likely to be in class with Hispanic students than with whites. At Altadena Primary School, for example, 64.3 percent of students were classified as Hispanic or Latino in 2011–2012 and 28.8 percent as African American. White students constituted only 2.2 percent of the school's population.[72] Washington Middle School was 85.2 percent Hispanic or Latino, 14.5 percent African American, and 0.9 percent white.[73] John Muir High School was 65.4 percent Hispanic or Latino, 29.5 percent African American, and 2.0 percent white.[74] The within school segregation that Del Yarborough had pointed out a decade earlier remained.

How different the composition of Pasadena's schools would have been without the busing-provoked white flight of the 1970s remains open to question. The influx of new students primarily of Mexican origin probably would have created a minority-majority school district even without the events of that decade. Nevertheless, it is clear that official desegregation did make a contribution to de facto segregation by helping to shrink the white numbers in the Pasadena public school system.

NEW YORK CITY

During the late 1960s and early 1970s, Southern political leaders accused northerners of hypocrisy for vigorously pursuing desegregation in the South, while schools and other institutions continued to be segregated in the north. In the nation's largest urban center, New York, schools were generally identifiable by race. The four boroughs of Bronx, Manhattan, Brooklyn, and Queens held roughly 600 public elementary schools in 1970, and half of these were either 90 percent or more white or 90 percent or more black. [75]

Lending support to Southern accusations, a New York state anti-busing law, passed by the state legislature in May 1969, sought to avoid judicially mandated racial balancing by specifying that only elected school boards could assign students to schools. The New York law, held unconstitutional by a federal court in October 1970, was widely copied by Southern school districts as a strategy for avoiding desegregation. [76]

The New York City boroughs made some efforts on their own to achieve racial integration through busing and school rezoning. These resulted in a number of conflicts. Responding to a plan by the Board of Education of Queens to rezone schools for more even racial combinations, the president of the Martin Van Buren High School P.T.A. declared, "They're talking about integrated schools. Well, they're going to have segregated schools. Because people will move out, that's all. Or put their children in private schools or parochial schools." [77]

In the spring of 1971, episodes of violence broke out between black and white students at South Shore High School in Brooklyn. [78] A mother and father of a public school student, who had fled the Soviet Union a few years earlier, complained about the treatment received by their son in a newly integrated school:

> Each school year he [the son] received certificates for his achievements. . . . This year, after attending school for two days in the sixth grade, he refused to go any longer. For participating actively in class, he has been called "Jewish faggot" and shot at with paper clips from catapults by his black classmates, because he "knows everything." . . . No teacher can start anything with students of such different ranges. . . . They [the black students] scatter the free lunches, preferring to extort food more to their taste—and money too—from their white classmates who are a minority and defenseless. [79]

The parents' characterizations of their son's black classmates were probably unfair generalizations from the behavior of a few, and one should be cautious about taking such reports at face value. The conflicts at South Shore certainly involved members of both racial groups and could have been sparked by white hostility. Still, these events testify to the disruptions of New

York's efforts at student redistribution, and concerns about the difficulties of teaching students with a wide range of preparation were well founded.

The earliest federal actions in New York were limited in scope. In January 1974, Judge Jack B. Weinstein directed the city's Board of Education to devise a rezoning plan to integrate Brooklyn's Mark Twain Junior High. Four months later, Judge John F. Dooling Jr. criticized the Board for allowing racial imbalances, and he ordered the members to redraw the boundaries of Franklin K. Lane School, also in Brooklyn, which was attended mainly by black and Puerto Rican students.

A local resident of the Lane school district agreed with the judge's decision, remarking that "over the years the Board has gerrymandered our area into an all-black school district." At the same time, though, the same man also observed that "the whites who got zoned in [to the Lane district] stopped sending their children to Franklin K. Lane and either sent them to Catholic schools or got addresses so they could qualify for other districts."[80] He did not, apparently, consider the possibility that rezoning would produce a rapid increase in false addresses and Catholic school applications.

Officials recognized the problem of segregated housing patterns. Judge Weinstein tried to tie the desegregation of Mark Twain Junior High to an effort to bring more whites into nearby housing projects. The Board of Education raised the possibility of reaching into the suburbs for whites. "Given shifting population patterns—the movement of the middle class to the suburbs—and the declining number of 'others' [whites] in the city's public schools," declared the Board in a report to the State Board of Regents, "the task of achieving meaningful integration within the boundaries of New York City or other large cities becomes increasingly difficult."[81]

Over the following years, desegregation in New York City proceeded largely on a school-by-school basis. To create greater racial diversity at virtually all-black Andrew Jackson High School in Brooklyn, for example, beginning in 1976 the Board of Education set up a special "choice of admissions" zone to encourage white enrollments and move black students elsewhere. The zone plan gave black children who would otherwise go to Jackson the option of selecting any schools in the city with white enrollments of greater than 50 percent (commonly referred to as "majority to minority" transfers).

At the same time, white students within the zone were required to enroll in majority black schools, limiting their choices of admissions. White students and their families were not cooperating with the plan. The *New York Times* reported that "many white students in these zones have chosen to attend private or parochial schools in the city or elsewhere."[82] The existence of other options for white students frustrated centralized planning.

Federal District Judge John Dooling recognized that the zone plan was not working at Jackson. Judge Dooling ordered the district to come up with another one in 1979. An appeals court overturned the judge's decision, though, on the grounds that Jackson and other city schools were becoming all minority because of changing demographics and residential patterns, not because of intentional actions by school officials.

An editorial writer, at that time, argued that the real problem was white flight to suburban areas. Therefore, New York should pursue a metropolitan solution, reaching into places such as nearly all-white Nassau County. The writer did not say how those pulled in from the suburbs could be restrained from doing precisely what the generally less economically advantaged whites within the city were already doing: leaving the public system. [83]

Meanwhile, the school boards of New York tried to engage in desperate juggling maneuvers to keep schools as integrated as possible, avoid over-crowding, and keep whites, who made up only 30 percent of New York students at the end of the 1970s, from fleeing the area. To relieve enrollment pressures on Intermediate School 231, and to minimize white flight, in 1978 the Queens school board created a new school, drawing students from the mixed-race, middle class neighborhood of Rosedale.

Rosedale had already been losing white residents, but the creation of a new, more middle-class school helped to slow down their departure. The president of the school board in school district 29 of Queens, Dolores Grant, explained that "white students were fleeing. That was a fact of life. It was not hearsay. The annex [the new school] helped turn that around."[84] Federal authorities would have none of the explanations of the Queens school board. On August 29, 1979, the Federal Office for Civil Rights gave the board thirty days to desegregate I.S. 231 or lose $3.5 million in federal education funds. [85]

The redistribution of white students from the mostly white Rosedale annex of I.S. 231 to the mostly black I.S. 231 provoked what may have been New York City's greatest desegregation controversy. During the summer of 1980, New York City Public School Chancellor Frank J. Macchiarola, pushed by the threat of losing funds, ordered that 450 seventh and eighth graders be transferred from the mostly white annex to the predominantly black main school. The transfer would result in white students becoming a minority of 15 percent in their new school.

In taking this action, the chancellor overrode the authority of local school board 29. The president of the local school board, Joseph Albergo, answered by saying that the transfers would result in over-crowding, as well as racial tensions. "No parent in his right mind will send his child to that school, especially under these conditions."[86] Ironically, the annex was one of the city's more integrated schools, since it contained about forty black and 330 white children, while many of New York's schools consisted solely of minority students. [87] An editorial writer at the time observed that:

The loss of more white students would make district 29 resemble more closely the many community school districts in New York City in which meaningful integration is no longer possible because of a dwindling white enrollment in the public schools, which citywide are now less than one-third white. Meanwhile, parochial and other private schools in the five boroughs, which have a combined enrollment of 312,647 are two-thirds white. [88]

The battle over the Rosedale annex took place in the courts and out. Parents of students in the annex, which was located within the mostly white P.S. 138 elementary school of Rosedale, sought to appeal the chancellor's order to the court, only to have the appeal dismissed early in 1981. Macchiarola came under additional pressure from the federal government, when, at about the same time as the dismissal of the appeal, the Federal Office of Civil Rights declared that the annex was illegal because it had resulted in the segregation of the main school. Angry parents in majority white Rosedale declared a boycott of majority black I.S. 231. [89]

The parents of students at the forbidden annex occupied the building and staged sit-ins. New York Mayor Koch barred their eviction, expressing some sympathy for the protestors and seeking a peaceful resolution to the problem. People in the neighborhood claimed that the closing of their local middle school and the transfer of their children to another neighborhood constituted a fatal assault on their community.

Joseph Albergo, the fiery school board head, declared, "They're [the Federal authorities and the city government] the ones doing the segregating. All these billions of dollars haven't done a thing, but our community became naturally integrated, and they want to destroy it."[90]

During the first week of February 1981, police officers swooped down on the Rosedale annex, evicted protestors, and arrested the few who refused to leave.

As word of the evictions spread through the community, about 250 demonstrators gathered in front of the school with homemade signs. Local parents declared that they would continue their boycott, and refuse to send their children to I.S. 231.[91] New York's Mayor Koch and Chancellor Macchiarola both criticized the protesting parents for their disregard of the law, believing that the protests had gone beyond disagreement with policy and turned into defiance of civic order.

Many black parents and several black officials were offended at the unwillingness of the Rosedale inhabitants to send their children to a school where whites would be a small minority and insisted that the Rosedale parents should follow policies established by the city and the federal government. Dr. Shirley Rose, a black school board member, declared that, "If they feel that the public school system cannot satisfy their needs they have the

right to go to private schools."[92] Responding to Dr. Rose, an assistant principal at Benjamin Cardozo high school observed:

> Unfortunately that [white, middle class movement to private schools] is pre-
> cisely what will happen. At a time when pressure is being put on Congress to
> pass laws that will bring about a voucher system and/or tax tuition credits,
> public education needs all the friends it can get. What is happening in Rose-
> dale is hastening the demise of the public schools. The middle class is being
> told it is not wanted. How can any system of public education function without
> the support of the backbone of its community?[93]

The people of the Rosedale neighborhood defended their protest marches
and sit-ins as desperate measures, intended to save a community centered on
its schools. Rosedale was a small, working-class enclave, surrounded by
poverty and urban deterioration. Mrs. Sandra Petker, an active PTA member,
explained that, "closing the annex would be the beginning of the end, abso-
lutely. Whites have been staying in Rosedale because of the schools. If the
community starts moving because of the closed annex, I'd have to move
too."[94]

By the beginning of the 1981–1982 school year, appeals to the courts to
re-open the Rosedale annex had been decisively defeated and the boycott had
come to an end. Reportedly, 10 to 15 percent of the students who enrolled at
I.S. 231 were white. Ironically, apparently as a consequence of desegregation, minority predominance at the school was sufficient to qualify the school
for a $300 million federal grant through the Emergency School Act to pro-
mote desegregation.[95]

We can never know for certain if retaining neighborhood schools would
have stemmed white movement out of the boroughs of New York or out of
the city public school system. All the indications suggest that maintaining
schools such as the Rosedale annex would have at least slowed the process.
This is counterfactual history, though, and there is no way to convince those
who prefer to believe otherwise. We do know that attempts to redistribute
students for desegregation did not desegregate the schools.

The proportion of white students in New York schools had gone down
from 30 percent at the end of the 1970s to just 15 percent in the 2002–2003
school year. This was slightly more than the 13 percent who were Asian.
Hispanics had displaced black students as the largest category in the city,
since 34 percent of those on the New York City public school rolls were
black in 2002–2003 and 38 percent were classified as Hispanic.

In the formerly white enclave of Rosedale, the Rosedale Elementary
school was 93.5 percent black and 4.8 percent Hispanic. P.S. 138, where the
Rosedale annex had been housed, was 88.9 percent black and 6.8 percent
Hispanic. I.S. 231 had become the Magnetech 231 Educational Center, offering special magnet programs. Two decades after it was a center of the deseg-

regation controversy in New York, this middle school was 90.9 percent black and 6.3 percent Hispanic.[96]

In a series of articles titled "A System Divided," published over several months in 2012, the *New York Times* examined the changing racial and ethnic composition of New York public schools. In this series, the newspaper provided a view of a school system in which non-Hispanic whites had become a small minority. Among the schools, a high degree of de facto segregation prevailed.

"In the broad resegregation of the nation's schools that has transpired over recent decades," wrote reporter N.R. Kleinfeld, "New York's public-school system looms as one of the most segregated. While the city's public-school population looks diverse—40.3 percent Hispanic, 32 percent black, 14.9 percent white and 13.7 percent Asian—many of its schools are nothing of the sort. About 650 of the nearly 1,700 schools in the system have populations that are 70 percent a single race, a *New York Times* analysis of schools data for the 2009–2010 school year found; more than half the city's schools are at least 90 percent black and Hispanic."[97]

The white students who remained in the system often did so, rather than flee to private schools or move to the suburbs, because they could find ways to avoid disadvantaged minority concentration schools through winning spots in elite public institutions through academic achievement: "New York has eight specialized high schools whose admission is based entirely on the results of an entrance exam."[98] Given the racial and ethnic achievement gaps that we will describe below, this meant that these schools had few black and Hispanic students.

At Stuyvesant High School, considered the best public school in the city, whites made up 24 percent of students in 2012, while blacks were 1.2 percent and Hispanics were 2.4 percent.[99] The elite public schools tended to be dominated by Asians, though, who generally lacked the ability of whites to flee to private institutions or leave for the suburbs. At Stuyvestant, 72.5 percent of students were Asian in 2012. Because of their dedication to studying in order to win places in the elite schools, though Asian students were only 14 percent of students in the system in 2011–2012, they made up 60 percent of those at the eight top schools with admissions based on test results.[100]

A system of meritocratic admissions will clearly continue to segregate students by race and ethnicity. Although the NYC Department of Education trumpeted the claim that "NYC students outperformed students in NYS [New York State] across student groups" on the new NYS common core tests in 2013, this "outperformance" was largely an artifact created by comparing the city's Asian and white students to Asian and white students elsewhere, even though white students made up a much smaller proportion of the school population of the city than of the state as a whole.

On that test, Asian students in grades 3 through 8, concentrated in a few magnet programs in NYC, scored at or above the proficient level in mathematics at a rate of 61.4 percent in NYC, while 60.3 percent of Asians throughout the state were at the proficient level in math. Among the white students, who were a small proportion of NYC's pupils found largely in the top schools, 50.1 percent scored at or above proficient in mathematics, compared to only 38.1 percent of white students throughout the state.

In English, the city's Asians (more often immigrants or children of new immigrants than Asians in other locations) did slightly worse than Asians in other parts of the state. Among NYC Asians, 48.1 percent were at or above proficient, compared to 50.4 percent of New York State Asians. Tellingly, one should note that Asians did better than even New York's white students in English, since 46.8 percent of whites in the city and 39.9 percent of whites throughout the state were at or above proficient.

The city's black and Hispanic majority, though, scored far lower than either Asians or whites, and no better than blacks or Hispanics elsewhere in New York State. In mathematics, 15.3 percent of blacks were proficient or better (exactly the same as the percentage of blacks throughout the state), and in English 16.3 percent of blacks were proficient or better (only slightly more than the 16.1 percent of statewide black students). Among NYC Hispanics, 18.6 percent were proficient or better in math, and 16.6 percent proficient in English (as opposed to 18.4 percent of statewide Hispanics in math and 17.7 percent of statewide Hispanics in English). [101]

It is interesting, although disconcerting, that in 2013 black students were still doing worse than any of the other groups; even worse than Asian and Hispanic students in English, despite the fact that many Asian and Hispanic students lived in immigrant, non-English speaking households. But it is clear why Asian and white students would be concentrated in the elite schools and programs throughout the city, and why their families would seek to avoid desegregation into mostly black and Hispanic schools if policy makers would ever recover the "political will" to make new aggressive efforts at racial redistribution.

Given the achievement gaps, being in a classroom with black and Hispanic students (and especially with black students) means being in a low-performing classroom. Those who want to avoid low-performing classrooms can either leave the system altogether, as whites did during the history of desegregation, or they can find schools that select on the basis of achievement within the system. Those schools will be racially identifiable, with mostly Asian and a substantial minority of white students.

INDIANAPOLIS, INDIANA

As in many other school districts, the desegregation fight in Indianapolis began in the late 1960s. In March 1967, the NAACP asked federal agencies to investigate the student assignment system of the Indianapolis Public School system. The following year, the U.S. Justice Department sued the system under the Civil Rights Act of 1964. Judge S. Hugh Dillin received the case. In August 1971, Judge Dillin ruled that Indianapolis was segregated by race.

The judge ordered school officials to come up with a plan to integrate. Two years later, the judge ordered that black students be transferred from Indianapolis to eighteen schools in the suburbs of Marion County, which contains Indianapolis, and several other counties. The other counties were later taken out of the decision by a Court of Appeals in Chicago. A two-person committee appointed by Judge Dillin drafted a plan that would involve busing 9,200 students.

With Indianapolis, the Supreme Court allowed another exception, along with Louisville, Kentucky, to its 1974 Detroit ruling (see the section on Detroit). The Indiana city had merged many of the governmental functions of Indianapolis and Marion County in 1969, leaving the school system as one of the few public services that had not become part of the merger. This led an appeals court to conclude in 1975 that not including the schools gave evidence of an intent to discriminate in the maintenance of districts and that busing between city and suburbs would not therefore be the kind of cross-district busing forbidden by the Supreme Court.

The desegregation plan was to be drastic. It would involve immediately transferring 6,500 black Indianapolis students in first through ninth grades to schools in the suburbs. These would be eventually joined by another 3,000 black students bound for the suburbs. Within the Indianapolis system, both white and black students would be bused. The Housing Authority of Indianapolis would be enjoined from building any new housing within the city's school district.

Despite the 1975 conclusion of the appeals court, the busing did not begin until 1981, when 5,600 black students were bused from schools within Indianapolis to the townships of Decatur, Franklin, Lawrence, Perry, Warren, and Wayne. Ten racially identifiable elementary schools and one high school were permanently closed. For a time in the 1980s, the Indianapolis desegregation plan did create just the kind of racial balances desired by the advocates of redistributing students.

However, these racial balances did not last. As the *Indianapolis Star* observed in 2004, "tens of thousands of students, most of them white, have either moved out of the district, or flocked to private, parochial, or charter schools in the area, disrupting the racial balance."[102] Within the schools, the transporting of students from city to suburb created the appearance of racial mixing at the school level, only to maintain racial segregation at the class-room level.

In a report on suburban Broad Ripple, the *Washington Post* observed in early 1998, that "Indianapolis' careful desegregation measures bring a mix of black and white students to Broad Ripple's door every morning, only to resegregate them all over again by the time they sit down for class."[103] Since admission to magnet programs was based on academic skills, the white students were concentrated in the resource-rich magnet program, while the black students were in the regular classes.

In 1998, the Indianapolis Public Schools and the six surrounding town-ships of Marion County signed an agreement to gradually end busing from the city to the suburbs over a thirteen-year period. As a part of the agreement, the Indianapolis Housing agency would help low-income families resettle in the suburban areas. After over thirty years of desegregation, massive school closures, millions of dollars spent on litigation, and acknowledged white flight from the public school system, "the city's schools are nearly as segre-gated as they were in the early 1970's."[104]

Even though high schools contain a wider variety of students than schools in the lower grades, because there are fewer of them in each district, the high schools in Indianapolis were still very racially segregated by the early twen-ty-first century, and most of the diversity in its high schools came from increases in the numbers of Hispanic students. Arlington High was 81 per-cent black in 2003 and 92 percent black in 2013. Broad Ripple was 76 percent black in 2003 and was 70 percent black and 10 percent Hispanic a decade later, despite the fact that it had become a magnet school for the performing arts.

Arsenal Technical was 68 percent black in 2003. Ten years later, Arsenal was 57 percent black and 19 percent Hispanic. Northwest High was 61 per-cent black in 2003. By 2013, the students of Northwest were 60 percent black and 20 percent Hispanic. Emmerich Manual High (which had become a charter school by 2013) was the only high school in Indianapolis that did not have a black majority in the twenty-first century, with a school population that was 58 percent white and 32 percent black in 2003, becoming 64 percent white, 16 percent black, and 14 percent Hispanic a decade later.

In the suburban districts around Indianapolis, many of the schools contin-ued to be identifiably white concentrations in the years following the 1998 agreement. Franklin Central High, in Franklin Township, was 90 percent white in 2003 and was still 81 percent white in 2013. Much of this slight increase in diversity at Franklin Central had come from new population groups, since blacks still only made up 6 percent of the students there in 2013. Another 6 percent of Franklin students were Hispanic, and 3 percent were Asian.

In Decatur Township, Decatur High was 88 percent white in 2003 and still 80 percent white in 2013 (Decatur High was still more diverse than the schools of Decatur township in general, which were 97 percent white). In Perry Township, Perry Meridian High went from 84 percent white in 2003 to 69 percent white in 2013. At Perry Meridian, though, the change was largely due to an increase in the Asian student body, since Asians were over 10 percent of the school's students in 2010, more than either blacks (9 percent) or Hispanics (7 percent).

Southport High, also in Perry, went from 82 percent white in 2003 to 61 percent in 2013. There also, though, the largest part of the increase in diversity came not from black students, but from a growing Asian population, since Asians, at 13 percent of Southport students, were the single largest non-white group.[105] The non-public school system that observers said had received the white flight during the desegregation years was also still flourishing immediately after the 1998 agreement. In 2000, one out of every five white students in the area, including the city of Indianapolis and the suburban regions, was in the non-public system, which was 82 percent white.

Desegregation, then, had not led to any meaningful change in racial composition of schools by the beginning of the twenty-first century. Most of the demographic change that had occurred, especially in suburban areas, was a consequence of rising numbers of Hispanic and Asian students resulting from international migration. Decades of desegregation had also not made much of an impact on racial and ethnic achievement gaps.

Within Indianapolis public schools, for example, only 40.3 percent of black students and 56.0 percent of Hispanic students passed both the math and English sections of the state's ISTEP achievement test in 2012, compared to 59.0 percent of whites and 69.6 percent of Asians. In the almost entirely white district of Decatur, by contrast, where too few minority group members took the test to be listed separately, 73.4 percent of white students passed both portions of the test in 2012. The decades since Judge Dillin's desegregation order had not seen any meaningful integration or educational equality either within or across the still racially identifiable school districts of Indianapolis.[106]

DETROIT, MICHIGAN

On April 7, 1970, the Detroit Board of Education adopted a voluntary plan of racial desegregation, to begin the following fall. Resistance to the plan on the part of the Michigan legislature led the NAACP to file a suit with the United States District Court the following August. The complaint maintained that the Michigan legislature and other officials had interfered with the plan for the desegregation of schools.

The NAACP further demanded a plan that would erase "the racial identity of every school in the system and maintain now and hereafter a unitary nonracial school system."[107] This was a tall order, since the public school system of Detroit was already composed overwhelmingly of black students in the early 1970s. In response to the suit, the United States District Court and later a Court of Appeals sought a metropolitan solution. The Detroit desegregation plan would combine the schools in Detroit, which were about 70 percent black, with 53 predominantly white districts in two suburban counties.

Supporters of the Detroit plan saw that in many urban areas the only way that any kind of a meaningful racial mix could be created would be by reaching out to take white students from the suburbs. "The outcome of the Detroit case," wrote one editorialist as the case reached the U.S. Supreme Court, "will materially affect school desegregation in other Northern cities. In Philadelphia and Chicago, for instance, there are not enough white pupils within the city limits to provide racial balance, and the neighboring suburbs are the only source of supply."[108]

The federal courts and the advocates for the metropolitan redistribution of students argued that respecting school district boundaries simply made it possible to maintain dual school systems that were separate, as well as highly unequal—and therefore unconstitutional. Further, many pointed out that school district lines were rather arbitrary lines on maps, and that there was no need to approach these as the natural order of nature. Opponents of metropolitan transfers objected that school districts were political entities.

Within a district, elected officials made educational policy. Moving students to other districts would essentially be placing them under the jurisdiction of school boards for which their own families and neighbors had no vote. Others argued, on practical grounds, that shipping busloads of inner city pupils out to the suburbs could either lead to greater sprawl, as white families sought to avoid the impact of widening desegregation, or to a wholesale abandonment of suburban school districts.

The Nixon administration inserted itself into the Detroit issue. Early in 1974, United States Solicitor General Robert H. Bork urged the Supreme Court to return the Detroit case to the United States Court of Appeals for the Sixth District for more evidence that there actually had been a violation of the Constitution that required busing across school districts.[109] On July 25, 1974, the Supreme Court rejected city to suburb desegregation in Detroit, with Justices Douglas, White, and Marshall dissenting from the majority opinion.

The Court observed that differing treatment of white and black students had occurred within the city's school system, and that therefore the city, not its politically separate neighbors, must come up with a remedy. Further, the high court ruled that the judiciary of the lower courts was taking as their own the power of elected representatives:

... it is obvious from the scope of the inter-district remedy itself that absent a complete restructuring of the laws of Michigan relating to school districts the district court will become first, a defacto "legislative authority" to resolve these complex questions, and then the "school superintendent" for the entire area. This is a task which few, if any judges, are qualified to perform and one which would deprive the people of control of schools through their elected representatives.[110]

Critics of the court's decision argued that it meant that desegregation could not be achieved in urban areas with predominantly black residents. Families throughout the districts that had faced the influx of central city students, though, reacted with jubilation. As one observer wrote, "In the suburbs of Detroit there were expressions of joy today, excited calling of friends to tell them that the Supreme Court had ruled that their school children would not be bused into Detroit."[111] Retrospectively, the notion that judges made bad superintendents was a prophetic one, and would be the cause for much grief in many subsequent desegregation cases.

In any event, the president of the Detroit school board, C.L. Golightly, realized that there was no way to desegregate a majority black school system. After the Supreme Court ruling, Golightly said that he saw no point in pursuing a desegregation plan for Detroit, since trying to spread the white minority around would simply result in an all-black system.[112] Despite misgivings such as Golightly's, after the U.S. Supreme Court struck down cross-district busing, U.S. District Judge Robert E. Masacio put a city-wide desegregation order into effect in early 1976.

Judge Masacio wanted to avoid provoking white flight from a city that was already losing its white population. Only 21,853 of the city's 247,500 students would be bused. White students, found mainly on the fringes of the city near suburban areas, would not be sent into the inner city, but would just exchange students with nearby predominantly black schools. No currently white school would be allowed to become more than 50 percent black.

While it is difficult to pinpoint the exact role played by racial redistribution in changing the school population, Detroit did subsequently lose nearly all of its white students. By the twenty-first century, demographics had made school desegregation impossible in Detroit, as in so many large American cities. Whites made up only 12 percent of all the people and only 7 percent of the school-aged children in Detroit in 2000. Nearly one out of four of the small number of school-aged white children in Detroit was in a private school in 2000, so that white students were a scant 6 percent of the public school enrollees in Detroit.

Detroit's twenty-first century problems as a city cannot be attributed to school desegregation. When Detroit became the largest U.S. city to file for bankruptcy in 2013, this appears to have been the long-term result of the loss of core industries, over-commitment to public pensions, and political corruption. But it is also true that Detroit, like other urban centers, had achieved nothing by its earlier desegregation efforts and had become a place in which any kind of desegregation was simply inconceivable.

The 2007–2011 five-year American Community Survey of the U.S. Census Bureau reported that 82.4 percent of Detroit's total population was classified as African American.[113] Detroit was socioeconomically as well as racially isolated. Over one-third (36.2 percent) of all those in Detroit and a majority of those below age 18 (50.4 percent) lived below the poverty level in 2007–2011.[114] Among Detroit public school students in 2009, 79.1 percent were classified as low-income and 88.2 percent were black. Whites made up a scant 2.5 percent of the district's students in that year.[115]

Over forty years after Detroit began attempting to desegregate its schools, the city also remained low-achieving. Results of the 2012–2013 Michigan Educational Assessment Program (MEAP) showed that only 7.8 percent of Detroit 11th graders were proficient or advanced in mathematics, compared to 28.6 percent of all Michigan 11th graders. While 53.5 percent of Michigan 11th graders reached the proficient designation in reading, only 35.1 percent of Detroit 11th graders ranked at this level. In science, only 4.1 percent of Detroit 11th graders were at least proficient, compared to 25.7 percent of their peers throughout Michigan.[116]

PRINCE GEORGE'S COUNTY, MARYLAND

U.S. District Judge Frank A. Kaufman ordered Prince George's County to begin busing students to achieve racial desegregation in December 1972, after black parents and the NAACP filed a lawsuit charging that the district was running a dual school system. At that time, approximately 78 percent of the public school students in the county were white. After this decision, though, the number of white students dwindled rapidly, so that whites were a minority a decade later.

By 1985, when 60 percent of the students were black, many of Prince George's schools were segregated again because it was difficult to find enough whites to integrate the schools. Recognizing that busing would only diminish the supply of whites still further, in 1985 the school district sought permission from the court to use magnet programs to draw white students into black schools. The special programs in fifty-three of the county's 180 schools provided resources not available in regular school programs, and a specialized curriculum that gave students opportunities to specialize in sixteen different themes, such as French, classical studies, and the arts.

In order to use these to pull in whites, though, the school system had to maintain slots specifically for white students in those schools, and to limit the numbers of blacks who would be allowed to attend. Using magnet schools to attract white students, rather than using forced redistribution of pupils seems, in theory, like a good way for schools to achieve racial balance. If, as we have argued here and elsewhere,[117] white avoidance of black schools is largely based on rational self-interest, then magnet schools may be seen as a way to make racially mixed schools attractive to white families.

Despite the advantages, though, there are four big, interconnected problems with magnet schools such as those in Prince George's County. First, if the value of an education is created more by the students in a school than by anything the institution can offer in the way of programs or curricula, then desegregation itself may undercut the value of schools, whether they are magnets or not. Second, to the extent that schools contain largely white magnet programs inside of predominantly black institutions, then magnets simply replace segregated schools with segregated classrooms.

Having within-school segregation may be preferable to having white students outside a system altogether, and not contributing to it, but it does not mean real desegregation and it raises a third problem. Maintaining places in magnet programs for white students means systematically discriminating against black students and denying places to them. It is therefore a strange way to go about correcting the effects of historical discrimination.

The fourth problem with using magnet programs to retain white students is that, like most strategies that aim at creating some desired mix of students, it deals poorly with changing demographics. If magnet schools work in attracting white students, then they essentially set a cap on the number of whites in a system. Magnets can retain as many whites as there are reserved seats; the number can go down, to the extent that the strategy does not work perfectly, but it cannot go up.

By 1996, the proportion of white students in Prince George's County had dwindled to less than 19 percent, whereas the percentage of black students had increased from 65 percent in 1985 to 72 percent of the county's public school population. The initial court order had mandated that no school could be more than 80 percent black. But this became increasingly difficult to achieve with so few whites available. So, as happened in some other desegregating systems experiencing white flight, like Baton Rouge, the court simply changed the goals.

In 1995, the court ordered that elementary schools could be no more than 86.6 percent black, middle schools could be no more than 90.8 percent black, and high schools no more than 90.3 percent black.[118] The magnet schools, meanwhile, had 500 openings for non-black students, but no one was available to fill them, while 4,100 black pupils were on waiting lists trying to get into the magnets. This led to an effort among some on the Prince George's school board to get the federal court to free the district from the 1985 mandate.

As school board member Verna Teasdale realistically observed, "in a school system that is 72 percent African American, we are not going to get enough white children to fill those slots."[119] Others on the school board, though, disagreed with Teasdale. As the *Washington Post* reported, "board members admit openly that they fear losing the millions of dollars—between $11 million and $16 million—they receive annually from the state to operate desegregation programs, which include the magnets."[120]

These other board members favored continuing to deny access to black students because of dependence on desegregation funds for a school system whose demographics had placed it beyond any possibility of true desegregation. In June 1996, the Prince George's school board voted by a five-to-four margin to ignore the 1985 court order and fill the magnet school positions with black students. In place of the magnet strategy, the board approved a "desegregation" strategy that created high achievement neighborhood schools over six years.

Extra resources would be given to schools that became one-race schools because of the make-up of their neighborhoods. The school board's attempt to act without judicial approval provoked a response from the NAACP, though, which filed a motion with U.S. District Judge Peter J. Messitte, who had been overseeing the case since 1994. Judge Messitte required the school board to apply to him before making any changes in the magnet plan.[121]

Thus, in this seemingly alternative political universe, we had the convoluted situation of black school board members elected by mostly black citizens who were unable to make decisions on behalf of black students, without obtaining the permission of a white judge. This united a usually divided school board, which voted unanimously in late July 1996 to ask Judge Messitte to lift the desegregation order that had been in effect since the early 1970s.

The school board asked the judge to replace the desegregation order with additional funds. Under the approach proposed by the board, the county and state would pay for a $346 million program to improve neighborhood schools.[122] Just where this money would be found was unclear, though, especially after county taxpayers voted for limitations on taxes at the end of 1996.[123]

During the summer of 1997, an independent panel appointed by Judge Messitte reported that Prince George's had done all it could to end school segregation. The following October, the school board and the NAACP, which had been at odds on the issue of ending racial quotas in the magnet schools, together drafted a plan to end the long desegregation suit over a three-year period, if the county and state would agree to provide $500 million to the school system. In view of the difficult tax situation, many legislators responded that this expensive proposal was unrealistic.[124]

Finally, at the beginning of September 1998, Judge Messitte ordered an end to the twenty-six year court-supervised desegregation of the district's schools. Over the following six years, busing would be phased out as the district built thirteen new neighborhood schools and upgraded old ones. The settlement required that Prince George's County concentrate on improving the achievement of all students and on closing the gap between black students and others. [125]

The white proportion of Prince George's public school students fell to fewer than 13 percent in 2000 and this proportion continued declining in the following years. The percentage of black students did decrease somewhat from the time of Verna Teasdale's remark, but only because of a dramatic rise in the numbers of Hispanic students. By 2013, the students in Prince George's County schools were 66.1 percent black, 24.2 percent Hispanic, 4.5 percent non-Hispanic white, and 2.9 percent Asian. [126]

Thus, the only large-scale intergroup contacts that were possible were between the black and Hispanic students who constituted over 90 percent of the district, a sharp contrast to the over two-thirds white school make-up at the time of the beginning of the desegregation effort. While it is difficult to estimate to what extent the change in the county's schools resulted from desegregation *per se* and to what extent demographic shifts occurred for other reasons, the history does suggest that desegregation played a large part in driving out white students.

A large racial and ethnic gap in achievement continued, in spite of the 1998 settlement. On the 8th grade 2013 Maryland School Assessment test, over one-quarter (29.7 percent) of the black majority in Prince George's County and about one-third (31.8 percent) of Hispanics scored in the lowest basic level in reading, compared to 16.6 percent of whites in the county. In mathematics, most black pupils (50.4 percent) and most Hispanics (52.2 percent) were in the basic category, compared to one-quarter (24.3 percent) of whites. At the other end, most whites (55.4 percent) scored in the highest, advanced category in reading and 39.1 percent were classed as advanced in math.

Only 14.8 percent of black students and 13.0 percent of Hispanic students were advanced in mathematics, and just 30.9 percent of blacks and 27.0 percent of Hispanics in Prince George's were advanced in reading. [127] Within each racial category, moreover, minority students in St. George's did less well than other Maryland students. [128] Regardless of how much other factors contributed to the county's minority concentration, Prince George's long desegregation struggle had not desegregated its schools in any meaningful way, and it had left intact the large racial achievement gap.

BOSTON, MASSACHUSETTS

In 1974, the Boston school district was found guilty of *de jure* segregation, and was ordered to implement one of the most ambitious mandatory student reassignment plans ever devised by a court. The plan ordered thousands of blacks from the northern part of the city bused to the southern part, and white students from South Boston ("Southies," of whom many were Irish-Americans) bused northward. Students being bused from their neighborhood schools could literally wave to other students being bused in from far away to take their places.

The district broke out in an orgy of nationally televised violence. Following rioting and bus burnings by incensed white parents, whites began fleeing the system by the thousands, never to return. By the time the Boston school system was declared unitary in 1989, it had lost most of its white students. However, race-based school assignments continued until 2000—as did white flight—until the practice was supposedly abandoned as a policy following a parent-initiated lawsuit.

However, the Boston school system was sued yet again in 2002 for considering the race of students in school admissions. Only this time, the school board was accused of discrimination against white, and not black students.[129] It wasn't until 2013 that the system completely abandoned the last remnants of its busing plan.[130] Despite the historical fiasco of redistributing students, the city still would not approve a component of the plan which would reserve 50 percent of all the seats at schools for children who lived within a mile of the school.

Some parents thought this plan would give an unfair advantage to those who resided near "good schools." Moreover, the district had to hire an MIT student to come up with a complicated computer algorithm to assign children to schools. One thing is sure though: most children in most schools will be poor and minority students regardless of the complexity of the computer model used. From 1990 until 2013, the number of majority minority schools in Boston more than doubled. The number of "intensely segregated schools" (from 90–100 percent minority) increased by 493 percent over the same period.

Race and socioeconomic status in Boston continued to be highly correlated a half century after America began its war to end poverty, especially among minorities. This correlation meant that the growing number of minority-dominated schools in Boston were also high poverty schools. In 2010–2011, the typical white Bostonian student attended a school that was only 22 percent low-income, compared to the typical black student who was enrolled in a school that was 59 percent low-income, and the typical Latino, who was attending school where almost two-thirds of his/her classmates were low-income.[131]

The percentage of white students in the average minority child's class-room in Boston decreased every single year from the beginning of forced busing in 1974 through 2013, during which time the system went from 57 percent to 13 percent white.[132] By 2013, minority students made up most of those left, since 36 percent of Boston's students were black, 40 percent were Hispanic, and 9 percent were Asian. Whites and Asians remained the high performers in the district (especially Asians). Despite their overall tiny repre-sentation, Boston's elite Boston Latin School (a grade 7–12 prep school) was 28 percent Asian and 48 percent white in 2013.[133]

The command and control approach to school desegregation of the type imposed upon the citizens of Boston was supposed to usher in a new social order of racial peace, harmony, and equality in this former abolitionist stronghold. Unfortunately, the social planners overlooked the fact that schools are not just expressions of political goals, but social environments embedded in American communities. Policies cannot succeed if they are inconsistent with the interests of individuals, social groups, and communities of those most able to make decisions in the educational marketplace. As a famous Bostonian once quipped, "All politics is local."[134] Unfortunately, the local context was most definitely not considered throughout Boston's long desegregation drama.

LOUISVILLE-JEFFERSON COUNTY

In the 1974 Detroit case, the U.S. Supreme Court had refused to allow cross-district busing, apparently closing the door on racially motivated busing be-tween suburbs and urban areas. However, the Court found reasons for flex-ibility on this principle in the situation of Louisville, Kentucky, where 52 percent of the students in the city of Louisville were black. There, a court had ruled that Louisville and surrounding Jefferson County, plus another district, if needed, should be included in a single plan.

The Sixth Circuit Court of Appeals successfully got around the Detroit precedent by ruling that both Louisville and Jefferson County had engaged in discriminatory practices together and that a single solution was therefore permitted. Before the case even reached the national high Court, the Ken-tucky state board of education merged the Louisville and Jefferson County districts.

However, the Court's acceptance of the reasoning of the Sixth Circuit Court made it possible for another small district, Anchorage, Kentucky, to be included in the redistribution of students. Under the plan to be enacted, 11,300 black students would be bused to the suburbs and 11,300 white stu-dents would be bused to the city. In the face of bitter local anger by some over the decision, United States District Judge James F. Gordon ruled in late

August 1975 that anyone attempting to tamper with school buses to be used in desegregation would face federal prosecution.

On September 4, 1975, Louisville and surrounding Jefferson County became the first metropolitan area in the United States to carry out busing for desegregation between city and suburbs. At a mass rally at the Kentucky State Fairground the night before, at least 10,000 protestors gathered to denounce Judge Gordon as a tyrant. A boycott by white students cut attendance on that first day to less than half of all students enrolled, and about 2,000 protestors defied the judge's orders against protest.

At Fairdale High School, in a working class white neighborhood in Jefferson County, about 200 demonstrators attempted to block buses leaving the school with black students. On the second day, violence broke out in the white working class suburb of Valley Station. Although most of the demonstrations around the metropolitan area were peaceful, about 2,500 demonstrators in Valley Station fought with the police, injuring as many as thirty officers. The police fought back with tear gas, arresting about seventy-five of the demonstrators. By September 10, the Kentucky National Guard had to be called in to stop the rioting and violence.

Although the struggle was long and hard, with the Louisville school system frequently accused of not living up to court orders, supporters of forced desegregation were optimistic about the long-term results. The Kentucky Commission on Human Rights issued a report in May 1977, claiming that the two-year busing plan had given families with school-age children an incentive to end housing segregation. The report maintained that the number of black families of pupils was increasing in the previously all-white suburbs and that in ten years busing could end because it would have achieved its ends. [135]

Within the schools, desegregation brought concerns. A survey of students in 1978 found that 63 percent of white students and 43 percent of black students believed that there were racial tensions in their schools. "Discipline problems have soared," observed one reporter. "White parents fear that the quality of education has declined, while black parents fear the loss of their community identity and institutions." [136] Segregation by classroom also continued, with white students in advanced classes acknowledging that they had no black classmates. [137]

By 1979, it was becoming clear that racial segregation was re-appearing at the school level, as well as at the classroom level, because white students were disappearing from the Louisville-Jefferson public school system. This led to efforts to re-adjust the transfers of students. School officials tried to blame the drop in white numbers on declining white birth rates, but parents, in contact with other parents who were making school decisions, disputed these kinds of dismissals.

Mrs. Jean Ruffra, a parent of two school-aged children, remarked, "what has happened, and the Central Board of Education knows it, is that we have white flight from the public school system. The figures are proof that it is true, and that is the reason they want to revamp the busing plan. Supposedly at the time, this was the best plan implemented in the country, and if it was such a good plan then, why isn't it anymore?"[138]

When Louisville-Jefferson County was finally declared unitary in 2000, the plaintiffs in the desegregation case were opposed because schools were still segregated at the classroom level. They argued that 53.1 percent of high school classes and 33.6 percent of middle school classes exceeded the guidelines that mandated each school to have no less than 15 percent and no more than 50 percent of students of one race. The court, however, responded that the school-level guidelines did not apply to individual classes.[139]

School attendance data from the 2000 census show that white students were a minority of 36 percent in Louisville public schools. This was because over one-third of the white students in Louisville were in nearly all-white private schools. An examination of tract-level data in 2000 shows that Jefferson County was still highly segregated residentially at the time unitary status was granted, in spite of earlier claims that school desegregation was changing racial housing patterns. Neighborhoods with large black populations tended to have few whites, and vice versa.

Since the U.S. Census will not give numbers when there are fewer than fifty members in a group, many Louisville tracts either listed no black residents or no white residents in divisions that ranged from about 4,000 to about 8,000 in numbers of people. Of the 170 census tracts in Jefferson County, 85 reported that there were fewer than fifty black residents and ten reported fewer than fifty white residents. This residential segregation appears even on a larger geographic scale. Among Jefferson County's eight large county subdivisions, the Jefferson Central region was 76 percent white.

Jefferson Northeast was 88 percent white, Jefferson Southeast was 89 percent white, Jefferson Southwest was 91 percent white, Louisville East was 93 percent white, Louisville South was 70 percent white, and Louisville West was 79 percent black. Only Louisville Central, located by the river with by far the smallest number of residents (about 31,000, or about one-third of the other sub-divisions) was approximately equal in black and white residents.

Four decades after the bitter conflict over desegregation and two decades after unitary status, black and white students continued to show highly unequal performance. The Kentucky Performance Report of 2011 showed that 58 percent of white non-Hispanic fourth graders in Jefferson County public schools were ranked as "proficient" in reading and 15 percent ranked as "distinguished," the highest of four levels.

By contrast, only 41 percent of African American fourth graders were "proficient" and only 5 percent were "distinguished." The lowest level of "novice" contained 18 percent of African American fourth-graders compared to just 7 percent of non-Hispanic whites. In mathematics, 38 percent of white fourth graders were in the highest of the four levels and 36 percent were in the next highest. Only 14 percent of the African American fourth graders were in the top category.

While 36 percent of African American fourth grade students ranked as "proficient" in mathematics (equal to the percentage of whites in this category), over one out of five (21 percent) were "novice" compared to 9 percent of white students. Among tenth graders, 21 percent of whites scored in the highest level in reading and 56 percent scored in the next highest category. By comparison, 7 percent of African American students were in the top level and 45 percent were in the second highest level. In the eleventh grade mathematics results, one-third of African American students (33 percent) were in the bottom achievement category.

Only 29 percent of the African American high school students scored "proficient" in mathematics, and only 3 percent ranked as distinguished. On the other hand, nearly half of white high school pupils (47 percent) made it into the "proficient" category and more than one out of every 7 (15 percent) was ranked as "distinguished."[140] In short, despite all the disruptive desegregation efforts of the 1970s, the schools of Jefferson County remained racially unequal in achievement in the twenty-first century.

Even after the Louisville-Jefferson County district was declared unitary in 2000, the district continued a "voluntary" desegregation plan that involved the use of race in making student assignments to schools. The district was sued by a white parent whose child was not admitted to her first choice of elementary school solely on account of her race. In a momentous Supreme Court decision in 2007 that we discuss in more detail in the companion volume to this book, the Louisville-Jefferson County district (along with the Seattle Washington school district) was found guilty of unconstitutional racial discrimination, and ordered to abandon its "voluntary" desegregation plan.[141]

CHAPTER SUMMARY

The brief case histories of desegregation failures that we assembled in this chapter have provided some insight into how attempting to redistribute opportunity through desegregation contributed to the de facto segregation of entire school districts. In some situations, such as in our first case in Baton Rouge, pressures to escape from the market controls of desegregation led to suburban areas attempting to split off from their larger districts. Some of the demographic changes, such as the increase in Hispanic or Latino students, were not results of policy decisions, but of larger changes in American society. However, shifting demographics simply illustrates that populations cannot be planned and redistributed.

We will follow these clear failures by considering a few districts that either have been described as successes or that were not unambiguously disastrous, such as was the case in Baton Rouge, Beaumont, or Boston. This next chapter will, revealingly, be shorter because the clear failures have been far more numerous and more obvious. We will see, though, that even the apparent limited successes were only illusions of success. Further, the districts in this next chapter continue to illustrate how individuals make their schooling choices within specific educational markets.

Chapter Four

Market Options and Illusions of Success

In school districts around the country, monopolistic, command and control desegregation approaches to the economic marketplace were followed by three outcomes: the abandonment of urban school public schools, suburbanization, and/or increases in private school enrollments. School desegregation was not the only factor in population shifts, since immigration, particularly of Hispanic populations, increasingly changed the racial/ethnic make-up of districts in ways that could not be controlled by governmental authorities. However, as we saw in case after case in the school districts in the previous chapter, it was simply futile and pretentious to assume that courts and planners can redistribute populations at will.

Readers may justifiably question, though, whether desegregation was a complete fiasco everywhere. What about the success stories? In this chapter, we will look at some of the "relative" successes, in which whites did not completely desert desegregating districts or in which districts or clusters of districts came up with plans that did seem to improve opportunities for some minority students. None of these were unqualified successes, in the sense that none of them resulted in truly desegregated education.

After looking at the illusions of success, we will consider why outcomes varied across districts. These outcomes differed, we will argue, because those who were able to make decisions about education had differing options in their educational marketplaces. Choices were constrained, but nowhere did these produce the egalitarian settings dreamed of by educational activists. Segregation among schools was often replaced by segregation within schools. Some minority students could get out of central city environments by voluntarily going out to the suburbs. But patterns of inequality continued to be deeply ingrained.

LITTLE ROCK, ARKANSAS

Little Rock was one of the earliest and most celebrated of American desegregation cases. It began before governmental attempts to redistribute students, when the goal was still to simply enable black students to enjoy the legal right to enroll in schools near their own homes. After the Supreme Court made its historic decision in *Brown v. Board of Education*, it appeared as if Little Rock schools would quietly follow the orders of the Supreme Court.

On May 22, 1954, the Little Rock school board announced that it would comply with the Supreme Court order as soon as the Court established a method and a schedule for desegregation. A year later, in May 1955, the Little Rock school board voted to adopt a policy of gradual desegregation to start in 1957. Under the plan devised by School Superintendent Virgil Blossom, Little Rock would first integrate the city's Central High School, and then gradually integrate lower grades.

The crisis broke out in 1957, the year that the school board had hoped to manage the quiet admission of a few African American pupils into white schools. Seventeen students were selected to be the first to break down the racial lines, but only nine of them decided to go ahead and enroll. Just before the beginning of the school year, on August 27, the Little Rock's Mothers League sought an injunction to halt integration.

The injunction was granted by Pulaski County Chancellor Murray Reed, but it was rejected three days later by Federal District Judge Ronald Davies. The enrollment of the African American students might still have proceeded in a relatively peaceful manner if the governor had not used the situation for political advantage. Arkansas Governor Orval Faubus was searching for political support to win a third term in office.

Governor Faubus decided that he could appeal to whites eager to preserve segregation. He declared that he would not be able to maintain order if Central High School were integrated, and on September 2 he ordered the National Guard to surround the school. His stand drew public attention to the situation and attracted white segregationist mobs into the streets. The next day, Judge Davies ordered that the integration of Central should continue.

The NAACP, under the local leadership of Daisy Bates, organized the African American students slated to enroll in Central High to arrive in a group. They were met by National Guardsmen who turned the students away with bayonets. One of the students arrived after the others and was confronted by screaming segregationists.

Television, which occupied a central place in most American homes by 1957, broadcast the scenes from Little Rock around the nation. On September 20, Judge Davies ruled that Governor Faubus had misused the National Guard to prevent integration and forbade the Guard's employment in this way. Faubus then replaced the Guard with local police. The nine black students entered Central High School through a side door on September 23. As they made their way into the school, an unruly mob of over one thousand people massed on the streets outside.

President Dwight D. Eisenhower met with Governor Faubus on September 14. Although the president believed that the governor had agreed to allow school integration to continue, it soon became evident that Governor Faubus had no such intention. Alarmed by the developments in his city, on September 24 Little Rock Mayor Woodrow Mann asked President Eisenhower for federal troops to maintain order.

Eisenhower responded by sending 1,000 troops of the 101st Airborne and then placing the Arkansas National Guard under federal control. The troops escorted the nine students to the school each day. Some Americans were shocked to see that military protection was needed to guarantee the basic rights of citizens. Others were disturbed at what they believed was a federal military occupation of a state, reviving historical memories of the military occupation of the South during Reconstruction, in the years following the Civil War.

The struggle continued even after the mobs in front of Central returned to their homes and jobs. On February 8, 1958, after several angry confrontations with white students, one of the nine, Minnijean Brown, was suspended for the rest of the year for dumping a bowl of chili on her white antagonists. Shortly after, the school board asked the federal court for a delay of the integration order until the concept of "all deliberate speed" was defined. The delay was granted in June and then reversed in August. In the meantime, the first African American student graduated from Central in May.

At the opening of the 1958–1959 school year, Governor Faubus ordered Little Rock public schools closed, and white students enrolled in private schools or in other districts. On September 27, 1958, Little Rock voters overwhelmingly rejected school integration. However, on June 18, 1959, a federal court declared that Little Rock's public school closing was unconstitutional. Little Rock schools opened a month early for the 1959–1960 school year and enrolled African American and white students.

Eventually, Little Rock calmed down, and for many Central High School became a story of the success of school integration. After opening its doors to students from all backgrounds, Central went on to become something of a showcase. In 1982, the *Los Angeles Times* proclaimed that Central was the best school in Arkansas, and that it had proved the critics of integration wrong. With a student population that was 53 percent black, it had fourteen National Merit semifinalists, and one of its black students had made the highest score ever recorded in Arkansas on the National Merit examination.[1]

While there is a great deal of truth to the success story, a realistic view will acknowledge that the success was not quite as clear and unblemished as sometimes claimed. In the decades after the Little Rock crisis, both the school district and Central High increasingly became concentrations of minority students. When President Bill Clinton made a celebrated visit to Central High in 1997, the year that the Little Rock school district was finally removed from court supervision, that formerly all-white school was about two-thirds black, and was heavily segregated internally

"Despite their overall numbers," observed *The Washington Post* during President Clinton's visit, "African Americans occupy just 13 percent of the seats in advanced classes and, in general, they tend to score worse, drop out more often, and draw more discipline than their white classmates."[2] The national newspaper *USA Today,* reporting on continuing controversies over school segregation in Little Rock, observed in September 2011 that many Little Rock schools remained segregated. *USA Today* wrote that "achieving racial balance is becoming more difficult as families leave the suburbs that supply white students to majority-black neighborhoods."

The newspaper quoted U.S. District Judge Brian Miller as saying that schools with minority students were plagued by low achievement and discipline problems.[3] In the 2012–2013 school year, 66 percent of all the students in the Little Rock School District were black. More than two-thirds of Little Rock students were below the poverty level, as measured by free and reduced price lunch eligibility.[4]

After the heroic struggles of black citizens to integrate Central in the 1950s, the most satisfying conclusion would be one of unqualified triumph. In a world that rarely follows the plots of good stories, though, the evaluation of events in Little Rock must be more measured. Simply striking down the barriers forbidding black students from enrolling in a local school did give them greater access to educational opportunities. This did not destroy Central as an educational institution, but it also did not create ideal racial balances in the school or eliminate substantial segregation at the classroom level.

Did the desegregating school districts that followed Little Rock, and which generally aimed at explicitly engineering racial balances, meet with better outcomes? Our sampling of some of the relatively "successful" districts suggests that there were many similarities with the consequences in Little Rock. It also suggests that there were many differences, though, and these differences raise serious questions about the wisdom of trying to manage the demographics of school enrollment.

CHARLOTTE, NORTH CAROLINA

Charlotte offers an important and interesting case for any survey of desegregating school districts. The Charlotte-Mecklenburg school system was historically significant because it began the national move to judicially mandated busing as a means of achieving desegregation. The district is even more worthy of a brief examination, though, because Charlotte acquired the reputation as "The City that Made It Work," and it was held up as a model for efforts at student redistribution throughout the nation.[5]

If, in fact, Charlotte was as successful as often suggested, we should look carefully at it and see why. Even if this were a case with a relatively positive outcome, though, it would be wise to be skeptical of claims that these outcomes could be repeated in other locations. Good public policy does not assume that exceptions can become the general rule.

The Charlotte-Mecklenburg school system dates back to 1959, when the city of Charlotte and Mecklenburg County, which contains it, voted to merge their two school systems. The system made some attempts to desegregate following *Brown*, and some black students did attend predominantly white schools in the region in the late 1950s and early 1960s. The schools were still largely segregated by race by the mid-1960s, though.

In 1965, Darius and Vera Swann sued the school district because their son, James, was not allowed to attend the school nearest his home, which was an all-white school. The Swanns, then, only wanted to send their child to a school in their own neighborhood. Ironically, their legal case would help to send hundreds of thousands of students away from their own neighborhood schools.

The Swann case went before Federal District Judge James B. McMillan. In April 1969, Judge McMillan issued his decision, arguing that neighborhood schools were discriminatory because black residents lived mainly in a single section of the city. Judge McMillan maintained that "as a group Negro students score quite low on achievement tests (the most objective method now in use for measuring educational achievement)"[6] as a consequence of attending all-black schools. The judge ordered the district to employ all means of desegregating, including busing.

The school board appealed Judge McMillan's ruling. The case reached the Supreme Court, and two years later the high court upheld the decision. The result was an explosion of similar desegregation plans. The 1971 school year opened with new plans for assigning students by race in over 100 school districts.[7]

Judge McMillan, the plaintiffs, and the school board came to agreement on a plan of action in 1974. The judge declared himself satisfied and removed the school from direct supervision, although the school board would have to continue to follow the 1974 plan. One of the key features of Charlotte's program was the pairing of elementary schools. A school in a majority white neighborhood would be paired with a school in a majority black neighborhood and enough students would be transported from each to create racial balances.

The desired racial mixture could frequently not be created with just two schools, so students were drawn from other locations, known as "satellites."

Most of the students who came from the satellites were black. This placed greater inconvenience on black students than on white, but most involved parties were convinced that sending white children into mostly low-income, black neighborhoods, would cause whites to leave the public schools. [8]

From the beginning, then, those in the Charlotte-Mecklenburg district carrying out school desegregation did recognize the possibility of white flight, and they made serious efforts to avoid it. The pairing strategy was not used at the junior high or high school levels. The higher grades had larger enrollments, so they drew on larger numbers of satellites. Again, these mainly came from black neighborhoods.

There was one important exception to the placement of satellites in black neighborhoods, though. White students in the well-to-do neighborhood of Eastover were sent into the formerly black West Charlotte. To make this palatable to whites, school authorities had to put new educational programs in West Charlotte. The district also re-drew the boundaries of West Charlotte so that these would include more middle-class black families and exclude many of the poor black families previously within the area.

Unlike many of the other cases in chapter 3, Charlotte did not lose its white students. The changes in the district's overall make-up during the years of aggressive desegregation were comparatively small. In the 1974–1975 school year, the system was 34 percent black. By 2001–2002, it was 42 percent black. Charlotte continued to retain its racial diversity during the first decade of the twenty-first century.

According to the district's statistics, in the 2012–2013 school year blacks still made up 42 percent of the overall population. Whites had indeed declined as a proportion, from just under 50 percent of the school population to 32 percent, while Hispanic and Asian representation had grown to 18 percent and 5 percent, respectively. However, changes in student make-up were gradual, and small enough to be attributed almost entirely to demographic shifts having nothing to do with the schools.

At first glance, then, Charlotte does look like the rare success story in school desegregation. It managed to put students of different races together in its schools. It did not cause whites to flee the system. There was no downward spiral in the quality of education in the district. A closer look, though, suggests that Charlotte does bear out the economic model of schooling that we described in the previous chapter.

White families did not leave the system, at least in part, because the district substituted segregated classrooms for segregated schools. Desegregation expert Roslyn Mickelson observed that "The Charlotte-Mecklenburg school system instituted widespread curricular tracking at the secondary level at about the same time that it began to comply with the Supreme Court's Swann orders to desegregate. Since the mid-1970s, the top tracks—those with the best teachers and most challenging curricula and pedagogy—have been overwhelmingly white while the lowest tracks have remained dispro-portionately black."[9]

At the end of the 1970s, the Department of Health, Education and Wel-fare (HEW) denied the school district a major grant on the grounds of exces-sive within-school segregation. By the early 1980s, Charlotte's schools ap-peared to have student bodies that were highly mixed in race. Beneath this appearance, though, a 1981–1982 survey of tracking in English classes showed that "in this district acclaimed for its desegregation successes, rela-tively few black students experienced a genuinely desegregated education, even in its showcase high school."[10]

Even with the segregation inside of schools, the institutions themselves tended to move slowly toward more racial separation. In a study of Charlotte schools from 1991 to 1993, the Charlotte League of Women Voters con-cluded, "the system appears to be continuing to drift toward blacker and whiter schools. Across the three year period, with few exceptions, the whitest schools got whiter and the blackest schools got blacker, whether they were elementary, middle, or high schools."[11]

At the beginning of the 1990s, the district largely replaced busing with a magnet school program as a strategy for achieving desegregation. Magnet school enrollments would be kept at 40 percent black and 60 percent white. This meant that whites, with (as we will see) much higher achievement levels than blacks, were limited in their access to magnet schools. White parents therefore sued the district, calling for unitary status and an end to race-conscious enrollment policies.

Nearly thirty years after the Charlotte-Mecklenburg system had made desegregation history, Judge Robert Potter ruled in September 1999 that the system had achieved desegregation, and he decreed that race could no longer be considered in school assignments.[12] With the end of judicial control, "the previous twenty year drift toward re-segregation accelerated markedly."[13] Students began to return to schools in their own neighborhoods, which were still largely black or white.

In 2009, looking back on the decade since the end of court-ordered deseg-regation, *The Charlotte Observer* noted that "in the ensuing decade, suburban schools became more numerous, more crowded, and generally remained higher performing. Last year about two-thirds of CMS's white students at-tended majority white schools in the suburbs. Center-city schools, including many magnets, have seen white and middle-class students dwindle. About two-thirds of the black and Hispanic students who make up CMS's majority attended schools where less than 25 percent of students are white."[14]

On the North Carolina Writing Assessment test for 2004, among CMS seventh graders, 62.3 percent of whites were in the top two levels, compared to 27.5 percent of black students. On the tenth grade portion of this test, 73.6 percent of whites and 41.8 percent of blacks were in the top two levels. On the North Carolina high school comprehensive test for reading in 2004, 82.2 percent of whites and 43.9 percent of blacks were in the top two levels. On the math test, the two top levels contained 84.8 percent of whites and 45.9 percent of blacks. [15]

The black-white achievement gap had been given by Judge McMillan as his reason for ordering desegregation by any possible means. The judge's mandate did not eliminate this gap. It continued to exist after desegregation had been in effect for nearly a third of a century.

Among the cases examined here, then, Charlotte-Mecklenburg did indeed have one of the most successful desegregation histories. The redistribution of students did not destroy the system. But neither did it end inequality in educational outcomes.

The only way families of children with relatively strong academic performance were willing to place their children into schools filled with children of relatively weak academic performance was through in-school racially segregated classrooms. Yet even then, like a centralized economic authority suppressing market forces, the authorities would have to use continual coercion to suppress individual choices. As soon as the judiciary removed itself from the school system, the schools began to re-segregate almost immediately and the re-segregation by neighborhoods continued over the years that followed.

MILWAUKEE, WISCONSIN [16]

When the Supreme Court handed down the *Brown* decision, citizens of Wisconsin generally regarded the Court's action favorably, but thought that it concerned other places. Wisconsin's laws, like those of several other northern states and in contrast to the laws of the South, prohibited segregated schooling. Several of Milwaukee's schools were about half black and half white, and the city's free transfer system made it possible for black children to enroll in predominantly white schools. [17]

During the 1950s, a boom in manufacturing drew black Americans from the South to Milwaukee at a rapid pace. Milwaukee's black population grew much faster than that of many other northern cities, including Chicago and Detroit. The recent migrants flowed into the center of the city, creating rapidly expanding black neighborhoods with residents of much more limited educational backgrounds than those of earlier black and white citizens.

In order to address the needs of newly arrived children with limited academic skills, Milwaukee schools in the late 1950s developed programs of compensatory education. These programs tended to separate the Southern-origin black students from others precisely because compensatory education was intended to address the special requirements of the migrants. School segregation, then, came from diverse educational needs, as well as from segregated housing and various forms of discrimination.

As Milwaukee's black population grew within the city center, so did the number of public schools with mainly black citizens. While there had been only seven predominantly black schools in 1950, there were an estimated twenty-three by 1964.[18] In the decade after *Brown* as the demand grew for schools that were truly integrated, and not simply open to enrollment without racial discrimination, many black citizens began to see the increasing number of mainly black schools as evidence of an educational ghetto.

When inner-city schools became over-crowded as a consequence of the rapidly increasing black population, the Milwaukee school board bused students from the crowded schools to other less-crowded schools, but it maintained a practice known as "intact busing." This meant that bused black students formed separate classrooms within white schools, a phenomenon that, in retrospect, ironically mirrored later decades' white magnet classes within black schools.

Opponents of racially identifiable schools joined together in the early 1960s under the leadership of civil rights attorney and NAACP president Lloyd Barbee. Barbee and his followers demanded that the school district place desegregation at the top of its agenda, integrate the intact busing students, and develop a comprehensive desegregation plan. When the school board delayed, the NAACP and its associates turned to protests and legal action.

During the mid-1960s, activists joined together to form the Milwaukee United School Integration Committee (MUSIC), demanding integration by marching and boycotting segregated black schools. Lloyd Barbee, the chairman of MUSIC and by now elected a state legislator, also acted as attorney in the desegregation case of *Amos v. Board*, filed in 1965 and supported in part by funds from the NAACP Legal Defense Fund. Long delayed by school board maneuvering, the case finally went to trial in September 1973.

While the case made its way through the court, there were efforts to resolve the situation by legislative means. Democratic Assemblyman Dennis J. Conta proposed, in the spring of 1975, that the state legislature merge suburban and city schools into a single school district. The mainly white suburban districts of Whitefish Bay and Shorewood, just north of the city, would be joined together with Milwaukee. At the high school level, this would make possible transfers among Milwaukee's Lincoln High School (94 percent black), Milwaukee's Riverside (61 percent black), Shorewood High (98 percent white), and Whitefish Bay High (99 percent white).

Assemblyman Conta proposed to use financial incentives to get the white schools to take minority students, and to cap transfer students at 20 percent of each student body in order to avoid white flight.[19] This recognition of the need to reconcile the divergent interests and motivations of different demo-

graphic groups held out some possibility of successful, if limited, desegregation. Conta's attempt to move desegregation from the federal court to the
legislature received insufficient support from his fellow legislators, though,
and this attempt at self-imposed metropolitan desegregation failed.

In January 1976, Federal Judge John Reynolds ruled that Milwaukee
schools were segregated and that the segregation had been intentionally established by the school board. The judge decreed that black enrollments
needed to be driven down between 25 to 45 percent in one-third of Milwaukee's schools during the 1975–1976 school year and to go down by a similar
proportion in the following two years. There was indeed substantial basis to
the declaration that the schools in Milwaukee were racially segregated. In
158 schools, over 100 were made up of more than 90 percent of a single
race.[20]

Judge Reynolds' demand was mathematically implausible, though. The
proportion of black students in the system had been increasing steadily, from
21 percent of students in the district when the suit began, to 34 percent by the
time of the decision. Projections indicated that black students would make up
50 percent of those in the district by 1980.[21] The judge does not seem to have
given serious consideration to the problem of making black enrollments at
specific schools go down rapidly when black enrollments overall were rising
at such a rate, or to the possibility that his own decision might speed up the
shrinking of white enrollments.

Following a second desegregation trial in 1978, the Milwaukee school
board began to make serious efforts at desegregation. The school system as a
whole did reach the predicted half-white, half-black composition in the early
1980s. This was largely due to the disappearance of whites from the city's
public school system, though, so it did not bode well for future plans to
distribute black and white students.

Although Assemblyman Conta's attempt at metropolitan transfers failed,
the state of Wisconsin did enact legislation to promote voluntary urban-
suburban desegregation throughout the state. Adopted in 1976, Wisconsin
Chapter 220 law provided extra funding to white suburban schools that
would accept black students from majority black districts. This program has
met with some criticism because it has been extremely expensive and, while
making it possible for some individual black students to have a wider range
of educational choices, it has tended to funnel money into already well-
heeled schools.

For Milwaukee, with the largest black population in the state, the program
also did not bring about any kind of desegregation. Even with Milwaukee's
Chapter 220 inter-district transfers, only 17 percent of Milwaukee's public
school students were white in the 2004 school year. Black students, at 60
percent, made up the majority. Hispanics, at 18 percent, were slightly more
numerous than whites.

Schools are generally judged to be desegregated if relevant racial or ethnic groups are within plus or minus 15 percent of their representation as a whole in the district. For Milwaukee, this means that when Judge Reynolds made his 1976 decision, any desegregated school would have been a majority white school, but at least one in five of its students would have been black. By 2004, though, a Milwaukee school could be considered "desegregated" if only 3 percent of its students were white. These are the paradoxical mathematics of racial redistribution.

As in other districts with large minority populations around the country, "diversity" came to mean more possibilities of contact between black students and the growing Hispanic population, since most of the whites had settled in the suburban fringe. In 2012–2013, Milwaukee public school students were 55.4 percent black, 24.0 percent Hispanic, and 13.9 percent white. Another 5.5 percent of students were Asian. A number of schools had almost no white students.

Carver Academy Elementary School, for example, was 91.4 percent black in 2012–2013. Congress Elementary was 94.4 percent black. Highmount Elementary was 90.1 percent black. Lincoln Middle School was 65.4 percent black and 25.3 percent Hispanic. The small Southeastern Middle School had only black students. Wedgewood Middle School was 91.9 percent black. James Madison High School was 93.0 percent black. Vincent High was 91.1 percent black.[22]

By 2013, the official literature on the Chapter 220 inter-district transfer described the program as aimed at giving minority students in the North, Central, and South Regions of Milwaukee the opportunity "to attend schools in suburban areas that are predominantly non-minority (white)." This would benefit only a limited number of individual minority students and was not intended to break down district segregation. The MPS literature warned potential applicants that "seats are limited in the Chapter 220 Program and no student is guaranteed a seat."[23]

The desirability of getting out of central Milwaukee and to the suburbs was clear. A planning document prepared by the University of Wisconsin-Milwaukee Employment & Training Institute in 2009 reported that "[i]n the 2008–2009 school year, 92% of MPS students attended a school where **over half of the children were poor** [bold in original] (as measured by eligibility for free lunch, or family income below 130% of poverty). Yet, only 4% of suburban and outer ring public school students in the four-county area were in school buildings where over half of the children were poor."[24]

Academic results reflected the concentration of minority students and socioeconomic disadvantage within Milwaukee. The 2009 NAEP results showed that Milwaukee students scored substantially below others in the state, in other large cities, and across the nation. These results also showed that racial achievement gaps remained. Only 28 percent of black Milwaukee

8th graders scored at or above the basic level in mathematics, compared to 61 percent of whites and 43 percent of Hispanics. In reading, 41 percent of Milwaukee black 8th graders scored at or above the basic level, compared to 78 percent of whites and 62 percent of Hispanics.

Within each racial/ethnic group Milwaukee 8th graders were less likely to be at or above the basic level than their peers in the rest of the state, in big cities throughout the country, or in national public schools.[25] Going to school in Milwaukee, rather than outside of it, greatly increased the probability that schoolmates would be low achievers. The more minority students in the classroom, the lower the general level of achievement, and the general level of achievement would be particularly low in a minority concentration classroom inside Milwaukee.

Individual minority families, then, had a genuine interest in getting to schools out in the suburbs. The Chapter 220 transfers, therefore, could provide good options in the educational marketplace for them. By the same token, though, families in the suburbs had a genuine interest in minimizing the flow of students out of the central city. As a consequence, the voluntary transfers could make greater educational opportunities to some, but they could not erase racial and socioeconomic inequalities.

ST. LOUIS, MISSOURI

St. Louis, along with Indianapolis and Louisville, was one of the few metropolitan areas where the effort to desegregate schools involved both the cities and the suburbs. It is an important case to consider because it is, along with Charlotte, one of the few that have been regularly singled out as one of the "success stories" of desegregation history. It began in the early 1970s, when a group of black students were reassigned from their neighborhood schools to less desirable locations on the grounds that their schools were becoming over crowded. The families of these students began a grassroots movement and initiated a lawsuit.[26]

On December 24, 1975, the case came before Federal District Court Judge James Meredith, who found that St. Louis schools were segregated by race. Judge Meredith issued a consent judgment and decree, directing the school district to take action aimed at desegregation. Sensitive to the fact that St. Louis was already losing white citizens to the suburbs, the judge did not order the reassignment of students or busing. Instead, the schools were to try to integrate their faculties by setting minimums for increases in minority teachers, and to use magnet schools to integrate student bodies.

Judge Meredith's decision was only an interim measure, because the case against the St. Louis School Board was still set to go to trial. The plaintiffs enjoyed the support of the federal government, after the Justice Department intervened on their behalf in 1977. At the trial in 1979, though, Judge Meredith found in favor of the school board. He concluded that the board had tried to create legally integrated schools by allowing all students to attend neighborhood institutions, and that segregation had occurred as a consequence of demographic shifts in housing.

Dissatisfied, the plaintiffs appealed. In March 1980, the Eighth Circuit Court reversed the 1979 ruling. Even though the court agreed that student assignments to schools had been racially neutral since the 1950s, the court found that the school board had failed to correct the results of legally segregated schooling incurred during the first half of the twentieth century. The school board, according to the court, had an obligation to create a school system without racially identifiable schools.

The case went back to Judge Meredith, who now approved an $18 million plan for desegregation within the district of St. Louis. A system without racially identifiable schools would be difficult to create solely within St. Louis, though, because only 23 percent of the district's students were white, and they were mainly concentrated in a single section. Court-appointed desegregation expert Gary Orfield wrote a report, pointing out that the suburbs would have to be involved in any attempt at meaningful desegregation.

In the early 1980s, then, the court began moving toward an inter-district remedy. A St. Louis-St. Louis County inter-district transfer plan took effect in 1983, with sixteen St. Louis County districts participating. The suburban districts had agreed to become part of this metropolitan solution out of fear that a federal judge would create a single district, encompassing the entire region. The transporting of students from city to suburb lasted for the rest of the century.

This finally came to an end in 1999, when the plaintiffs to the lawsuit, the state of Missouri, the Justice Department, the sixteen districts, and the St. Louis Board of Education finally came to an agreement to end the case. At that time, about 12,000 city students were attending schools in the county, and about 1,400 suburban students were traveling each day to the city. With the end of the case, inter-district transfers were to continue under a voluntary desegregation plan run by the Voluntary Interdistrict Choice Corporation (VICC), which allowed participating black students to move out of schools in the city to suburban schools. [27]

Many have celebrated St. Louis and its suburbs as a great success in school desegregation. Speaking before the House of Representatives in 1999, Representative William Clay announced:

> I want to call the attention of my colleagues to the remarkable story of desegregation in St. Louis. St. Louis illustrates the gains that can be made for children even in these times. In St. Louis, a 1983 settlement of a desegregation case brought by the NAACP resulted in the largest voluntary metropolitan

school desegregation program in the nation, with 13,000 black students from St. Louis attending school in 16 suburban districts. The program was very successful in increasing the graduation and college-going rates of participating youngsters as was a magnet program in city schools. [28]

An examination of the results of over thirty years of busing raises questions about the basis for this celebration. Economist Joy Kiviat, in 2000, observed that eight out of ten students in the city of St. Louis were black. Most were attending schools that contained virtually no whites. Per pupil spending came to $7,564 ($10,450 in 2014 dollars), but the dropout rate was 62 percent and students scored at the bottom on standardized tests. One-third of the public school teachers in St. Louis chose to send their own children to private schools, and private school attendance was above that of the national average, especially among relatively high income families. [29]

Data from the Missouri Department of Secondary and Elementary Education supports Kiviat's bleak view of St. Louis schools. According to this information, 82.3 percent of the students in St. Louis City public schools were black in 2013. Whites, who had been a little under 18 percent in 2000, had gone down to just under 12 percent of the student population in 2013. On the 2013 Missouri Assessment Program tests, 61.6 percent of Missouri white seventh graders and 45.5 percent of St. Louis City white seventh graders were proficient or advanced in English language arts, compared to 32.7 percent of Missouri black seventh graders and just 22.0 percent of black seventh graders in St. Louis City.

In mathematics, 64.6 percent of white seventh graders statewide and 32.1 percent of white students in St. Louis were proficient or higher, but only 33.7 percent of black seventh graders throughout the state and 21.9 percent of black seventh graders in St. Louis City were at this level. [30] The small number of white students in the city showed poorer outcomes than whites elsewhere in the state, and the black students in this minority concentration district showed worse results than both black and white students throughout Missouri.

The suburban districts that have received students from St. Louis varied in their racial compositions. The students of Webster Groves, adjoining St. Louis, were between 12 and 22 percent black in 1982. [31] By 2013, Webster Groves was still racially identifiable as a majority white district, with whites constituting 74 percent of students and blacks 19 percent of the student population. Black students in Webster Groves did better than their St. Louis counterparts, since 43.2 percent of black seventh graders were proficient or advanced in English language arts in 2013 and 56.3 percent were proficient or better in mathematics.

Nevertheless, there was still a huge racial achievement gap in the comparatively high-performing suburban district of Webster Groves, since 81.2 percent of same-grade whites were at least proficient in English language arts and 83.2 percent were at this level in mathematics. The Rockwood district, farthest from St. Louis, with a black student population under 4 percent in 1982, had become 12 percent black and 84 percent white by 2004 and 10 percent black, 80 percent white, and 6 percent Asian by 2013. In this still majority white district, the race gap was also great.

Only 34.6 percent of its black seventh graders in the Rockwood district were at least proficient in English language arts in 2013, compared to 76.6 percent of whites and 89.7 percent of Asians. In mathematics, only 30.0 percent of black seventh graders were at least proficient, while 79.6 percent of whites and 95.3 percent of Asians were proficient or better, according to the Missouri Department of Elementary and Secondary Education.

The best that one can say about the supposed St. Louis success story was that it was not a complete disaster. Since the whites in the suburbs were never forced to send their own children into the inner city, and busing from the city to the suburbs never inundated the latter, white families did not move en masse to private schools or leave the metropolitan area. The minority of black students who did go to school away from their own neighborhoods may have benefited from advantageous socioeconomic settings, although the cursory test results just cited suggest that this requires more study.

Desegregation in St. Louis can be judged a success only in comparison to the utter fiascos of many other locations, though. The years of inter-district busing and billions of dollars in transportation and administrative costs did not accomplish any of the stated goals of the program, though. These years did not do away with racially identifiable schools or racially identifiable school districts. Neither did this Herculean effort eliminate the enormous racial achievement gap, in either the city or the suburbs.

WHAT HAPPENED IN THESE DISTRICTS?

In these two chapters, we have taken these short case studies from desegregation cases around the nation. Some of the districts included here are in large, old industrial cities. Others, such as Dallas and Baton Rouge, are in post-industrial, mostly suburban metropolitan areas. More importantly, though, the districts showed outcomes that varied in desirability. The first set of case studies were clear failures at desegregation. Those in this chapter have been more ambiguous and have included some districts that have been lauded as success stories.

A closer look at the case studies suggests that these all involved responses to market pressures in different contexts. One is struck by an essential sameness that runs throughout. In none of these districts did desegregation really seem to work out as intended. Despite the general similarity among the districts, we can identify some patterns. These patterns occurring in history are strikingly similar to what we suggested would result from schools as markets of exclusivity.

In a number of the locations in both chapters, attempts to redistribute students were followed by the near total abandonment of entire districts by whites. The huge public school system of New York, the nation's largest classic urban area, became an almost entirely minority school district. Even little pockets of white representation such as Rosedale, ironically more racially integrated than the city as a whole, were wiped out. Chicago and Milwaukee, also old industrial centers, became cities in which white students were extremely rare.

Some may argue that whites left New York, Chicago, and Milwaukee for reasons that had nothing to do with the schools, that this was simply a reflection of white abandonment of the cities for the suburbs. Undoubtedly, schools were not the only cause of movement to the suburbs. However, such a defense of coercive desegregation policies would be strange indeed. Essentially, such a defense maintains that the policies would have worked, if only demographic realities had been more cooperative.

The claim that schools had nothing to do with suburbanization rings hollow, though. Repeatedly, parents proclaimed that they were leaving desegregating districts because of their school situations. Later, the same groups of people who said that they were leaving because of desegregation were gone. Surely, one has to consider the possibility that actions had something to do with clearly and unambiguously stated intentions. In addition, the abandonment of desegregating districts was not only a movement from central cities to suburbs. Largely suburban districts, such as Los Angeles, Dallas, and Baton Rouge, also lost their white students.

All of the districts that saw whites moving across district lines had at least one characteristic in common: there were other places to go. In this respect, the urban-suburban question was relevant. Moving out of New York or Chicago, or settling in a suburb upon moving to one of these metropolitan areas, meant that the disproportionately middle-class white families could put their relatively well-prepared children into schools with other children who were academically well-prepared.

Those who moved had the ability to exercise their options, and they understood that schools were markets of exclusivity. In suburban schools, their children were more likely to be surrounded daily by others who saw higher education as a natural next step and who did reasonably well on most measures of academic achievement. Movement from cities to suburbs, though, was only a part of the general search for places with better schools, as well as safer, more comfortable neighborhoods.

Most of these locations did see white movement out of desegregating districts. In many cases, this was also followed by middle-class black movement and "bright flight." In some situations, though, whites and middle class blacks did remain in school systems. Little Rock High School, opened to black enrollment before the era of coercive redistribution of students, became a majority black school, but it did retain a substantial white student body. Charlotte, a critical district in the history of coercive desegregation, actually retained a large white proportion even with its busing program. Why, then, wasn't there white flight from these places?

Part of the answer is that there were few more desirable options in the educational marketplace. Charlotte was not surrounded by potentially desirable school districts, and it included the school area of Charlotte-Mecklenburg. Districts that did not have competing districts had effective monopolies, in which the educational product could be manipulated and customers would still be likely to consume it.

The limitations on choice in these districts suggest that efforts at metropolitan desegregation were based on a sound approach that would have made good sense to John D. Rockefeller. If there is a challenge to a monopoly, extend the monopoly to include it. The problem with this reasoning is that if the perceived quality of the product goes down enough, the customers who have the mobility and financial resources will travel pretty far for an alternative. In Indianapolis, the historical testimony indicates that whites moved beyond the distant reach of the metropolitan public schools. However, in Charlotte, efforts were made to keep in-district public school options attractive to white parents, by limiting the busing of their children and providing segregated educational options within schools.

A variation on the inter-district approach might be to keep the educational markets essentially segregated by geography, while giving a small number of disadvantaged students access to the better schools. The number has to be kept small, of course, because large influxes of the disadvantaged would change the quality of education in the better schools. This was essentially the kind of metropolitan strategy employed by St. Louis and by Wisconsin's Chapter 220. This is good for individual black students who want out of minority-concentration schools. But it does nothing to change racial balances or to re-design American society.

Even when a wide geographic area is included in the educational monopoly, this still does not shut down all alternatives to the mixed schools intended by judicial desegregation. Private and parochial schools continue to compete with the public school system. As the value of public school education goes down with redistribution, those who can make the sacrifices become more willing to pay the costs of private education.

The districts we have considered here generally have very high rates of private school attendance. Parents said that they were moving to private schools in order to avoid desegregation. In the case of Baton Rouge, we have been able to document massive white movement into non-public schools, and indeed the creation of non-public schools, immediately following a judge's order to redistribute students by race.

Both the shift to private schools and the shift to other public districts have clear financial implications for desegregating districts. Those whose children attend non-public schools basically pay for education twice. They pay tuition where their children actually attend and they pay taxes for the public schools their children do not attend. It is not surprising that areas with high private school enrollments frequently have difficulty raising taxes for school spending. This makes the problem of inequality in school funding even greater, with minority students often on the losing end of the educational equation.

School districts that already have poor schools because they enroll students with limited preparation for schooling are further penalized by restricted funding. Parents in one district are generally reluctant to have their money shifted to another district. Sermons about the duty to treat all young people equally may induce guilt. But they will rarely succeed in getting people to agree to spend less of their money on the preparation of their own children and more of their money on schools their children cannot attend.

Finally, moving from one public school district to another and enrolling in private schools does not exhaust all of the options. The value of an education is established by classmates. Since there is a large and continuing achievement gap between black and white students, under most conditions families likely look for classes composed mainly of whites, although race would certainly be irrelevant in a class that contained top-notch students from all racial groups. When de facto segregation between schools is reduced by redistributing students, then segregation within schools tends to be one of the results.

Magnet programs, gifted and talented programs, and other kinds of elite public school education are often criticized as providing private schools inside of public schools. But if those kinds of special offerings were not available, the students in them would leave the systems. In addition, magnet and related programs must be elite in character. They must be restricted to those with high levels of academic achievement in order to attract and hold the best students. If they just offer unusual and interesting areas of instruction then they will attract a wider range of students and the educational quality will go down.

Magnets that are filled through test scores tend to be mainly white (or Asian), as a result of the test score gap. Thus, Little Rock's Central High, a shrine to the history of school integration, still has segregated classes as a result of tracking. When magnets drop achievement as an entrance requirement and attempt to hold on to white students by guaranteeing them places through quotas, this creates new problems.

Offering selective programs as a supposed tool for desegregation becomes a means of intentionally giving whites access to special resources, while systematically denying equal treatment to blacks. If the quality of the programs is not maintained by restricting entry to the highly qualified, whites can frequently find better educational products elsewhere. As in Prince George's County, school systems end up keeping black students out of magnet classrooms in order to hold open places to attract white students who are not coming.

Behind these stories of districts, then, we can see families making choices about educational products, the value of which is established by exclusivity. If they can, members of a middle class family will move into a neighborhood with a highly reputable public school, paying a higher mortgage than they may pay elsewhere. It is a good school because it is attended by children from their own neighborhood, all of whom have relatively good preparation and come from families who are actively seeking educational advantages.

To say that a school is a good one is to say that it is better than others, since good is a relative quality and schools are necessarily in competition, if they are not to sink into a general mediocrity. When a judge or other authority begins to redistribute the advantages and disadvantages of schools, by redistributing students, the good school is no longer so desirable. The family begins to look for other ways to give children an education that will prepare them for a highly and increasingly competitive society.

As in Beaumont, the family may put its home up for sale and move where there is no forced redistribution. Or, it may do a "virtual" move, entering an educational black market by seeking a false address for school enrollment. Or, it may leave the public system altogether and go to the private sector, where the costs may be greater, but where there is no pretense of equality. Or, instead of moving segregation upward by abandoning a public school district, families may move segregation downward, by demanding tracking and honors classes in order to retain their competitive advantages while participating in the illusion of redistribution.

CHAPTER SUMMARY

There are a few districts in which desegregation has been celebrated for its success. As this chapter has described, though, the success stories often involved a great deal of wishful thinking, as in Little Rock, which many were eager to see in a positive light because of its historic importance. In Little Rock, as in Charlotte, though, segregation across schools was largely replaced by segregation within schools. In other locations, such as St. Louis, metropolitan areas did hold on to white students even though St. Louis was one of the few locations where mandated desegregation across urban and suburban regions occurred.

The white students of St. Louis did not leave public schools or the metropolitan area, though, largely because schools remained racially identifiable in spite of efforts to redistribute by race. Milwaukee has provided an example of another kind of desegregation program that might be seen as a success, because of a voluntary inter-district transfer program that has enabled central-city minority students to attend suburban schools. Here, also, we see only the illusion of success because most Milwaukee minority students remained in segregated urban schools.

We have argued that the supposed success stories show the same underlying patterns as the other districts. Families that were in positions to make educational choices would seek internal segregation, through tracking or magnet programs, when this was a better option than fleeing a district or moving to a private school. But they would seek the best situations for their own children by whatever means were available, and this consistently undermined true desegregation.

If desegregation has failed because it has treated schools as monopolies and overlooked their character as competitive markets in which people make choices based on their social and financial resources, this raises the question of how choice might be included in school policy. This is a highly relevant question because some of the most hotly debated policy reforms today are market-based approaches intended to extend choice to more people. In the next chapter, we look at how today's choice-based programs, charter schools and vouchers, emerged from desegregation and face the same issues of school quality and equality that came out of desegregation.

Chapter Five

The Educational Marketplace and the Rise of the School Choice Movement

Calls for school reform have been almost a constant in the history of American education. In the post-World War II period, these calls have been expressed as the "why can't Johnny read?" plaint of the fifties and the "rising tide of mediocrity" worry of the eighties. With the equalizing social movements of the late twentieth century, which would include school desegregation efforts, the pursuit of equity became, along with the continuing chase after the elusive goal of excellence, a central theme in educational reform. Indeed, the primary justification for George W. Bush's 2001 No Child Left Behind Act, as stated in the law's concise preamble, is "[to] close the achievement gap with accountability, flexibility, and *choice* [italics added] so that no child is left behind."[1]

The pursuit of educational equity for racial and ethnic groups began with the prohibition of de jure segregation proclaimed by *Brown*. When this failed to equalize educational outcomes, active desegregation through the redistribution of students became a dominant policy. The redistributive efforts also failed, though, because they treated education as a monopoly. These policymakers failed to recognize that education is a market of exclusivity in which those able to make choices pursue the self-interest of their families.

The most recent efforts at school reform can be understood as continuations of one long-standing goal. This is to improve educational quality, while simultaneously responding to the educational disadvantages of schools and school districts that cannot be desegregated following decades of mandated redistribution of students. One obviously cannot redistribute white and minority students in locations that have almost no white students. This fact has played a large part in the most recent school reform strategies: charters and vouchers. In fact, one could say that these market-oriented strategies are a

101

sort of logical next step in addressing educational inequality, given the spec-
tacular failures of the heavy-handed command and control desegregation
strategies forced on schools and school districts.

Charter schools and school vouchers are attempts to improve the performance of students through competitive, market-oriented approaches to education. The charter school strategy attempts to increase competition among
schools by enabling chartering entities to set up a variety of types of schools.
Each charter school independently produces its own curricular "products"
under the broad oversight and assessment of school boards or other governmental agencies. Vouchers, on the other hand, seek to provide educational
subsidies to families of students to enable those families to make their own
school choices among public and private institutions. Although in theory
vouchers could go to all families of school children, these subsidies have in
actuality been directed to low-income students in traditional public schools
judged to be failing. Vouchers, like charter schools, then, aimed to employ
marketplace subsidies to redistribute educational opportunities.

Part of the impetus for these market reforms of education came from late-
twentieth-century perceptions that America was becoming less competitive
economically because the nation's students in general were not adequately
educated. A related notion held that teacher unions and strong tenure laws
had resulted in lax attitudes among public school teachers who would apparently work harder if there were more of a competitive element to the teaching
profession. However, charters and vouchers also had deep roots in struggles
over segregation and desegregation.

Some of the earliest attempts at these different ways of improving school
choice were aimed at enabling whites to choose segregated school environments in the immediate aftermath of the 1954 *Brown* decision. When years of
government-mandated desegregation did not produce truly desegregated
schools or equality of educational opportunity across racial and ethnic
groups, though, some school reformers began to embrace charters or vouchers as alternative ways to improve schooling for pupils in socioeconomically
disadvantaged, minority-dominated schools and districts. School choice went
from a means of avoiding desegregation, to a way of addressing the failures
of school desegregation.

In the twenty-first century, policy makers, journalists, and scholars continued to debate whether strategies for school choice would intensify segregation, break down segregation, or enhance educational opportunity for minority students in situations of unavoidable de facto segregation. Based on
the nation's experience with desegregation, though, we suggest that advocates of charters and vouchers are correct in seeing education as a competitive marketplace, but that they have generally failed to see just how this
marketplace works. Schools do not compete only on pedagogical approaches
or resources.

If educational outcomes depend on the students who attend schools, then schools do not compete to attract the largest numbers of pupils. Instead, they compete to get the most prepared and academically advantaged students. Part of the problem of the school choice movement, then, is that it is still haunted by assumptions and moral imperatives of the failed desegregation movement.

DESEGREGATION FRUSTRATION AND THE RISE OF CHARTERS

William C. Knaak and Jean T. Knaak have noted the rapid spread of charter schools, from 1991 when Minnesota passed the first charter-school law to 2013 when more than 5,600 charter schools existed in thirty-nine states.[2] This rapid increase is picking up speed as even more locations embrace the charter idea. Knaak and Knaak attributed this rapid spread to five main causes.

First among these causes was the perception by liberals that public education had failed to solve problems of racial and socioeconomic inequity. Second, many Americans believed that the United States was falling behind other nations economically because of inadequate education. Third, philanthropic organizations tended to focus on projects with clear expectations of results. Charter schools and vouchers, designed to respond to measured success on tests, often attracted philanthropic funding.

The increase in charters was driven, fourth, by the perception that charter schools would provide families with greater choice and control. Finally, media attention focused on highly successful charters, especially highly successful charters serving poor and minority students. Both the first and the last causes on this list clearly make charter schools direct products of the school desegregation movement.

Charter schools have been expected to take up precisely the tasks that desegregation was supposed to have performed. At the same time, the element of choice dealt indirectly with what we have argued was a primary reason desegregation failed to perform those tasks: federally mandated desegregation took choice and control away from the families of the most advantaged students. Advocates of school choice programs often did not see the potential conflict between choice and the goals of desegregation. Critics of those programs often failed to see why ignoring choice had defeated desegregation goals in the first place.

Knaak and Knaak discussed explicitly how the charter school movement emerged from frustration with efforts to desegregate schools. They noted:

> Members of Congress, who initially passed President Johnson's Elementary and Secondary Act of 1965 for the benefit of minority races and poor children, became increasingly frustrated with public schools. Most of this frustration related to the perceived and widely publicized seeming inability of the public

schools to meet the politicians' expectations of equity in academic education, especially for non-Asian minorities and the poor. Today, this thrust for equity has morphed into demanding the same test score levels for all races on standardized tests of academic achievement. The current disparity on standardized tests is referred to as the learning gap. As it became apparent that massive busing and forced desegregation were not going to solve the problem of the racial gap in learning, school district personnel created magnet schools where White, minority, and poor students could choose to attend together. Next, minority and poor students were allowed to choose any school within the school district. Then, they were allowed to choose places in schools in suburban school districts. The initial ESEA of 1965 and subsequent reauthorizations of that act up through the last reauthorization, known as No Child Left Behind (NCLB), had impressive bipartisan support in Congress. Yet nothing much has changed in the learning gap between White and non-Asian minority students since 1988, and the failures are largely attributed to ineptness in the public schools.[3]

Although many supporters of charter schools and other market-oriented reforms do see these as ways of improving education for all students, these types of reforms have, in fact, been directed disproportionately toward minority students. To illustrate this, Figure 5.1 shows enrollments in traditional public schools and charter public schools in the 2010–2011 school year. Although whites have historically declined as a proportion of the public school population, they still constituted a slight majority (53 percent) of all students in traditional public schools.

By contrast, whites were just over one-third (37 percent) of charter school students, in spite of the fact that the overall pool of white students was greater than that of pupils from any other category. Blacks were only 16 percent of traditional public school students, but 29 percent of those in charter schools. The rapidly growing Hispanic (Latino) school population was not as heavily over-represented in charters as the black school population, but Hispanics still constituted 28 percent of charter students, while they constituted 23 percent of those in traditional public schools. Most students in charter schools (57 percent) were black or Hispanic.

As we will see in the section below on the rise of school charters in specific districts, charters grew from the 1990s into the 2010s not simply as a strategy for improving general performance, but also as a means of addressing ongoing concerns related to majority-minority school districts. For example, how could minority performance be improved in districts with too few non-minority students to attempt equalization through redistribution of students? How could school districts create special programs to retain dwindling non-minority populations?

By the 2010s, charter schools were becoming a common and officially supported answer to these questions. President Barack Obama's Race to the Top initiative continued the push toward school choice, especially through

Traditional Public Schools

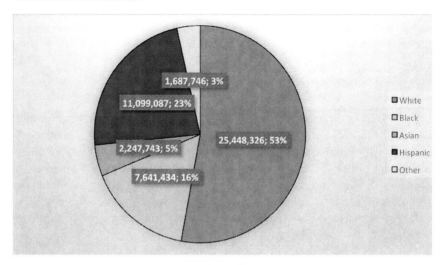

Charter Public Schools

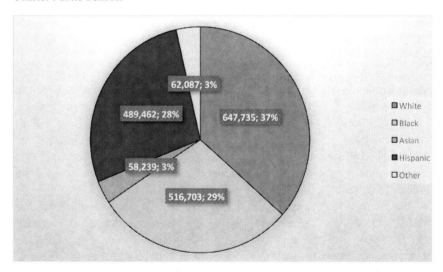

Figure 5.1.   Numbers of Students in Traditional and Charter Public Schools, by Race and Hispanic Ethnicity, 2010-11. *Source:* **U.S. Department of Education, National Center for Education Statistics, Common Core of Data (CCD), "Public Elementary/Secondary School Universe Survey," 2010–11.Table E-81.**

charter schools, as a way of simultaneously improving and equalizing education. In June 2009, Education Secretary Arne Duncan declared that in the competition among states to design educational plans that would win Race to the Top money, "states that do not have public charter laws or put artificial caps on the growth of charter schools will jeopardize their applications under the Race to the Top Fund."[4] So, tellingly, we see that the federal government has shifted from mandating student redistribution, to mandating school choice options.

MINORITY STUDENTS AND VOUCHERS

School voucher programs have grown less rapidly than charter schools. The essential idea of the voucher is that public funds may be given to families of students who choose how to employ those funds. University of Chicago economist Milton Friedman was probably the best-known proponent of vouchers. Friedman argued as early as the 1950s that American public schools were monopolies and were beset by the typical problems of monopolies: the provision of low-quality products that consumers must purchase because they have no alternative.

Although often referred to as a libertarian, Friedman did not suggest that government should get out of the business of education altogether. Instead, he proposed to employ governmental means to break down the government monopoly in schooling by subsidizing attendance at schools chosen by families.[5] Today, the Friedman Foundation for School Choice remains an active proponent of vouchers.[6]

During the late 1970s and 1980s, advocates of vouchers began to see possible allies in urban minority communities. Voucher proponents began to appeal to many African Americans and members of other minority groups, arguing that vouchers offered a way out of concentrated underachievement in socially isolated schools. On the eve of President Reagan's election, the Heritage Foundation circulated a policy paper that argued that inner-city minority parents, faced with declining schools that desegregation had done nothing to improve, could be attracted to voucher programs.[7]

Since vouchers would support attendance at religious as well as secular private schools, the idea attracted religiously based support, as well as support based on the presumed capacity of vouchers to improve education through competition. James Forman argued that many of the early efforts to secure public support for private school tuition through vouchers or tax-credit proposals were based on religion. Forman noted, however, that by the time the Supreme Court decided school vouchers were constitutional in the 2002 *Zelman v. Simmons-Harris* case, "the dominant argument for school vouchers rested on racial justice, not religion or values."[8]

Vouchers by the 2000s were aimed primarily at offering subsidies to disadvantaged students, most often members of minority groups, to enter the competitive educational marketplace and move out of traditional public schools with low achievement records. The idea of moving pupils out of institutions of concentrated disadvantage and into other institutions clearly employed much of the logic of desegregation, although vouchers expressed this logic in terms of enabling rather than enforcing movement, and attempted to expand the redistribution of students to private institutions.

The No Child Left Behind Act of the administration of President George W. Bush was the key piece of legislation in making the voucher movement a successor to the desegregation movement. As we pointed out in our 2009 history of American education, "closing the racial and ethnic (Latino) achievement gap and achieving universal equality among categories seemed to be a primary focus of No Child Left Behind."[9] One of the ways in which this equality would be achieved would be through enabling students to transfer out of schools judged to be failing, including through the use of vouchers to transfer to private schools.

Under the Bush Administration, Congress created the first federally funded and administered voucher program in 2004 in Washington, D.C. The program enabled low-income students in low-performing schools to transfer to private schools. This subsidization of educational competition had substantial local support within the largely minority community of Washington.[10]

Although the administration of President Barack Obama viewed charter schools favorably, as we saw in the previous section, this latter administration took a less positive view of vouchers, which it viewed as taking funds out of the public school system, and it attempted to cut funding for vouchers. However, Congress voted to maintain the D.C. voucher program, which provided money for transfers to private schools almost entirely to minority students in a district which, in total, was 69 percent black and 16 percent Hispanic in 2013–2014, with 77 percent of all students classified as low income.[11]

THE SPREAD OF SCHOOL CHOICE REFORMS

As charters and vouchers became the latest educational campaigns, many of the school districts we discussed in chapters 3 and 4 turned to choice-based reform efforts. Frequently, choice-based reforms were attempts to improve schools in districts where performance had declined as white flight had left concentrated minorities behind. Such reforms were also adopted to meet parental demands based in the same kinds of rational self-interest that had encouraged white flight and minority frustration.

In Little Rock, a symbolic location in the school desegregation movement, the Arkansas Board of Education approved a charter for the Little Scholars of Arkansas (LISA) Academy for enhanced math and science edu-

cation in 2004.[12] In the following years, charter schools opened throughout
Little Rock and Pulaski County, in order to retain the diminishing white
population and to improve achievement among black students, who continued to lag far behind.

North Carolina, where the great experiment in judicially mandated busing
began in Charlotte-Mecklenburg, turned to charter schools as the new effort
at school reform in 1996, when the state legislature approved up to one
hundred charters. By 2011, demand for enrollment in charter schools was so
great that the legislature lifted the 100 school cap. In the Charlotte-Mecklenburg area, dissatisfaction with the district's public schools fed demand for the
growing number of charter institutions.[13] This development, we believe, is
indicative of the district's less-than-stellar desegregation experience, which
is becoming more evident given that the charter school option is weakening
the monopolistic grip of the district. Prior to having this option, parents had
to accept the traditional offerings provided by the Charlotte-Mecklenburg
district.

The Dallas Independent School District, which had become an almost
entirely Hispanic and black system by the 2012–2013 school year, had become one of the nation's leaders in the turn to charter schools. In order to
attempt to improve the dismal performance record that we have documented,
the district turned to market-based reform. *The Dallas Morning News* reported in late 2012 that the Dallas ISD had enrolled more than 20,839 students in charters in the previous years.[14]

We have also examined the failure of desegregation in Chicago. By 1995,
the Chicago school system had reached such a deplorable state that Mayor
Richard Daley created the position of chief executive officer for the entire
system and appointed educational reformer Paul G. Vallas to that post. Vallas, who would later become known for overseeing a massive system-wide
experiment in charter schools in New Orleans, used charter schools as one of
his initiatives to attempt to improve education for the city's almost entirely
minority student population.[15]

By 2012, charter schools had become a key strategy in the campaign to
improve the schools of Chicago. The 119 charter schools in the city made up
most of the charter schools in Illinois, serving a student population that was
95 percent minority and 91 percent low-income.[16] In the wake of monopolistic attempts to redistribute, Chicago had turned to aggressively promoting
choice among schools.

In Texas, Beaumont had lost almost all of its white students during the
years of mandated desegregation and saw a decline in school performance.
Its turn to charter schools was not as intense as that of Dallas or Chicago.
Beaumont began to open charter schools by the beginning of the twenty-first
century following the Texas legislature's approval of charters in 1995. In
2001, Principal Brenda Lewis of Beaumont's Eagle Project charter school

pointed out the school's long waiting list as she observed that "parents are desperate for solutions and want other options for their child's education."[17]

Although school desegregation is often thought of as having begun in the South, our sections on Los Angeles and Pasadena described how, from the early 1960s to 1970, that movement extended also to the West Coast. In the succeeding years, Los Angeles became a mostly Hispanic school district with a large black minority and very few non-Hispanic white students. As the charter school movement grew in Los Angeles and throughout California, promoters of the school choice movement touted this as a way to get low-income minority students out of their racially isolated, underachieving schools.

In 2006, Alan Bonsteel, president of California Parents for Educational Choice, described inter-district transfers, voucher programs, and the conversion of traditional public schools to charters as ways to either get students out of racially segregated schools in LAUSD or to improve their options. Among the three approaches, Bonsteel argued that "allowing existing public schools to convert to charter status will probably work most quickly and help the greatest number of students."[18]

By 2013, charter schools had become a major feature of the Los Angeles educational landscape. The Los Angeles Unified Public School District had the largest number of students in charter schools in the United States, with 137,000 pupils enrolled in 248 Los Angeles charters in 2013. This was over one-fifth of the students in this second largest school district in the United States.[19]

Within Los Angeles County, the Pasadena Unified School District had, as we have seen, become a majority Hispanic school system by 2013, with a substantial black minority and with many of the remaining white students concentrated in racially identifiable white classes. Pasadena's adoption of charter schools, though, was more limited than that of the neighboring Los Angeles Unified School District.

As of 2013, the school district was home to three charter schools, and several other charters had opened and closed. Serving mainly low-income black and Hispanic students, charters in Pasadena, as in many other locations, focused primarily on improving performance in de facto segregated settings. As we have seen, these settings had emerged from decades of judicially mandated integration.

Pasadena saw the failures and closures of several charter schools over the years. However, the district received special attention when Pasadena Rosebud Academy, opened in 2007, posted particularly good test scores. "As the nationwide achievement gap between black, Latino and white students expands," proclaimed the *Pasadena Star-News*, "one Altadena charter school seems to be defying that trend, notching test scores that rival schools in neighboring affluent communities."[20]

On the opposite side of the nation from Los Angeles County, New York State authorized charter schools in 1998, but the school choice movement only began to take off in New York City under the administration of Mayor Michael Bloomberg. From 2003 to 2013, the total number of charter schools in the city grew from eighteen to 183. In 2012–2013 New York had the second largest number of children in charter schools in the nation, after Los Angeles.[21]

The city's greatest problem with underachievement lay with black and Hispanic students and with the de facto segregated schools those students usually attended. Accordingly, charter schools, as a strategy for improving student performance, were most visible among segregated black and Hispanic pupils. One New York charter school advocate noted that while 6 percent of all the city's public school students attended charter schools, "[i]n neighborhoods such as Harlem, where better educational options are most needed, the figure is as high as 33 percent."[22]

The rapid increase in charters and their prominence made this educational strategy a topic for debate in the city's 2013 mayoral election. The question of how competition among schools affected equality of distribution of educational resources gave a special local relevance to the national conversation about school choice, segregation, and opportunity. We discuss the arguments in this controversy in the following section.

In Milwaukee, eight out of ten public school students were black or Hispanic by 2013. Many schools were essentially single-race institutions despite the Chapter 220 inter-district transfer program and other continuing desegregation efforts. Milwaukee was also at the forefront of choice-based reforms. Vouchers, generally spreading much more slowly than charter schools throughout the nation, began with the Milwaukee Parental Choice Program in 1990–1991. This program provided vouchers to low or modest income families in Milwaukee to attend private schools at state expense.[23]

Milwaukee also opened a range of charter schools in hopes of improving the performance of its students. By 2013, local leaders at meetings hosted by the Metropolitan Milwaukee Association of Commerce were proposing following the Louisiana model, which we will describe in this section, by creating a Recovery School District. As in Louisiana, this RSD would take the lowest performing schools away from the school district and turn these schools over to charter school operators.[24]

In May 2001, Indiana became the thirty-seventh state to pass legislation to permit charter schools. The mayor of Indianapolis became the first mayor to hold authority to grant school charters.[25] Indiana was also second in the nation, after Ohio, in its use of school vouchers.

The largest number of Indiana vouchers were issued in Indianapolis and its surrounding Marion County, which accounted for 30 percent of Indiana vouchers in 2012–2023.[26] Income limits on vouchers and the claim that charters enabled students to move from failing schools to successful schools established clear linkages between some of the goals of desegregation and the goals of choice-based reforms. As in other locations, charters and vouchers were clearly ways to extend choice in the educational marketplace to those who had the fewest options.

In 1974, the Supreme Court had ruled that Detroit could not bus students to and from surrounding school districts to achieve desegregation in Detroit's already mostly minority schools. By the second decade of the twenty-first century, there were almost no white students left and the bankrupt city had become a concentration of low-income, low-achieving minority students. Faced with this situation, the district turned to charter schools as a way to improve performance.

By the 2012–2013 school year, Detroit was one of two cities (the other was New Orleans) that had a majority of public school students attending charter schools. Whether the charters actually had improved performance was a matter of debate: critics pointed to evidence that 73 percent of Detroit's charter schools performed below the average Michigan school. This criticism may have been misplaced because all Detroit students, regardless of school type, performed worse than others in the state.[27] In any case, Detroit was one more district that had turned in desperation to choice strategies following the decades of desegregation struggles.

In 2003, Maryland passed a charter school law. By the 2013–2014 school year, the mostly black and Hispanic students of Prince George's County in Maryland could opt out of their traditional public schools by enrolling in one of eight charter schools. Demand for the latter was greater than the supply, though, and a seat in a charter depended on a lottery system.[28]

Massachusetts introduced its first fourteen charter schools in 1995, two years after Governor William Weld signed the Education Reform Act. The legislation primarily aimed at committing resources to schools and at enacting stricter accountability measures for schools. Charter schools were included almost as an "afterthought," according to Governor Weld's later account. However, charters became a major focus of school reform over the following two decades.[29]

By 2014, thirty-six charter schools served Boston's mostly black and Hispanic student population. These schools competed for students by offering special programs. The Academy of the Pacific Rim, for example, concentrated on China-related studies. This 5th through 12th grade school taught Mandarin in every grade from 7th on up and had a China exchange program. Interestingly, given the heavy Asian concentration we saw in Boston Latin, this China-oriented school was only 3 percent Asian, while 60 percent of its students were African American, and 21 percent were Hispanic.[30]

KIPP Academy Boston Middle School explicitly declared serving lower-income and minority students as its mission. In 2014, fully 87 percent of its students were eligible for free or reduced price lunch and 99 percent were African American or Hispanic. Like other KIPP (Knowledge Is Power Program) schools, this middle school aimed to prepare disadvantaged students for college through a highly structured curriculum. [31]

Boston's Neighborhood House Charter School offered a curricular program of Rich Structured Learning Experiences to its 1st through 8th grade students, along with low student-teacher ratios and attention to special education. As in most other charter schools, Neighborhood House had mostly low-income and minority students. The school's website describes its student body as 82 percent minority and 65 percent low-income. [32]

Other charter schools in Boston provided similar specialized offerings. After years of tumultuous and tragic attempts to redistribute by command and control, there were no longer enough socioeconomically and academically advantaged students left for population redistribution. The competitive diverse provider system was not just the result of a market-oriented ideology, but a response to the utter failure of a scheme of equalization forced from above.

School choice reform efforts had not made as much progress in Louisville-Jefferson County schools as in the other districts we have examined. Kentucky was one of only eight states in the nation without legislation to permit charter schools. However, proponents were actively seeking to establish this type of education. Kentucky charter school advocates specifically praised charter programs such as the Knowledge is Power Program (KIPP), which were targeted primarily at lower-income, minority students.

The Kentucky advocates pointed to the black-white gap in achievement as a reason to turn to charters. In August, 2013 a charter school summit held in Louisville promoted charters as a way to respond to the needs of economically disadvantaged students in underperforming schools, which had been among the issues that desegregation had been designed to address. The Black Alliance for Education options was one of several sponsors of this summit. [33]

The schools of St. Louis, Missouri, were highly segregated after years of court-mandated desegregation, despite continuing attempts to send black students out to the suburbs through voluntary transfers. In 1998, dismayed at the low performance of students in the major urban areas, Missouri authorized charter schools for St. Louis and Kansas City. Beginning in 2006, St. Louis Mayor Francis Slay turned to aggressively promoting charter schools "to provide parents with a reason to stay in the city rather than move to suburban school districts," according to the *St. Louis Post Dispatch*. [34]

THE SPECIAL CASE OF NEW ORLEANS

Some of the most notable and nationally influential political programs for school choice reform have taken place in Louisiana, a state that we examined in detail in a previous book on the troubled history of school desegregation. [35] Prior to the Bayou State's experimentation with charter schools, desegregation in the capital city of Baton Rouge stretched from 1956 until 2003. Eighty miles south, New Orleans attracted national attention when federal marshals had to accompany six year old Ruby Bridges to a formerly all-white school.

Louisiana's charter school system began in 1995 when the state established a pilot program to allow school districts to open charter schools. Two years later, the state expanded the program by permitting the state school board, the Board of Elementary and Secondary Education (BESE), to act as an authorizer for charter schools. [36]

In 2003, the Louisiana legislature established the Recovery School District, a special statewide entity that would take over chronically failing schools and attempt to turn these around. The schools to be taken over by the RSD were minority-concentration schools, mostly in New Orleans, but also in Baton Rouge, with a very small number of schools located outside of those two districts. New Orleans was a focus of the RSD because it had one of the worst school systems in the nation.

By the end of the 2004–2005 school year, sixty-eight of the 105 Orleans Parish public schools were ranked "academically unacceptable" (failing). In that year, following the decades of white flight that we documented in our book on Louisiana desegregation, 93 percent of the students in New Orleans schools were African American (many of the non-black students were Vietnamese) and 77 percent were classified as low-income. In 2004, the overwhelming majority of children (83 percent) in the poor households of New Orleans lived in single-parent households, with most (78 percent) living with single mothers. [37]

After Hurricane Katrina hit the city in late August 2005, charter schools became the center of the recently begun attempt to reform schools. The relative independence of charter schools provided a way to re-open desperately needed schools quickly. Subsequently, observers who viewed the New Orleans experiment in school reform frequently opined that the hurricane, although an undeniable tragedy, had created an opportunity because it wiped out so many failing schools.

To head this educational experiment, the Recovery School District brought in as its first new head Paul G. Vallas, who had led the charter-heavy effort to reform Chicago schools. New Orleans steadily increased its investment in the charter enterprise over the following years. In 2008, 55 percent of the city's students were attending charter schools. By the fall semester of 2013, this had increased to 85 percent of students. Only ten of the city's eighty-eight public schools were non-charters.[38] At the beginning of Fall 2014, the Recovery School District of New Orleans became the first district in the nation to have only charter schools.[39]

The overall quality of New Orleans schools, as measured by test scores, does seem to have improved following the turn to a charter system. Although New Orleans schools still had a high failure rate on the state's School Performance Scores (SPS), test results were markedly better than before the transformation into a district of charters. On ACT tests, as well as on the SPS, schools in New Orleans showed greater improvement than those elsewhere in the state. The six New Orleans schools that made the state's list of High Performing-High Poverty schools were all charters.[40]

This apparent improvement in quality, though, came at the cost of inequality. In addition to the high performing schools, the city also had the worst schools in the state and some charters had closed because of poor achievement and mismanagement.[41] This, though, is precisely what one would expect in a competitive system. Competition means inequality. Moreover, implicitly conforming to the educational marketplace as a market of exclusivity in clientele, the schools were competing for students.

The New Orleans schools that were able to attract the most highly motivated students moved forward in this competitive market. Other schools fell behind. Advocates of market-based educational strategies who have represented these strategies as mechanisms for promoting greater equality (a goal from the desegregation heritage) have missed this essential point. Not only does competition tend to create winners and losers and thereby intensify inequality, but competition for students tends to sort students unequally.

While New Orleans became a national focal point for the charter movement, Louisiana as a whole became heavily involved in the other major type of choice-based education, school vouchers. In 2008, the state established its voucher program for students in New Orleans. This program enabled families with incomes less than 250 percent of the federal poverty level whose children were in public schools rated C, D, or F to be eligible for vouchers to attend private schools.

Although not earmarked specifically for minority students, in effect nearly all of the eligible New Orleans students were African American. In 2012, the Louisiana Scholarship Program of vouchers was expanded to the entire state.[42] Again, because of the strong correlation between minority race, low school ratings, and low income, this statewide program served chiefly minority (black) students.

SUMMARY OF RATIONALE FOR USING CHARTERS AND VOUCHERS FOR REDISTRIBUTION

School districts across the nation, then, turned to charter schools primarily for two reasons. One of these reasons echoed the earlier use of magnet schools as a desegregation strategy: school officials in places such as Little Rock and St. Louis believed they could retain white and middle-class students in districts with large proportions of low-income minority students through offering special options. The other reason was to try to improve performance in school districts that had become isolated concentrations of minority disadvantage in the face of the de facto segregation that judicial desegregation had failed to eliminate and that we have argued judicial desegregation in reality unintentionally exacerbated.

Voucher programs had spread less rapidly, but their links to segregation and desegregation were also clear. Voucher funds were directed primarily to low-income students for purposes of equalizing educational opportunities. As in desegregation efforts, vouchers aimed to achieve this equalization by redistributing students, most often minority students, from schools regarded as undesirable to schools regarded as desirable, although the redistribution through vouchers had the goal of moving students to private schools, rather than to public schools with different racial compositions.

THE DEBATE OVER CHOICE

Although supporters of charter schools and vouchers argued that these strategies would improve equality of educational opportunity for minority students, opponents maintained that choice would deepen historical inequalities by enabling whites to separate themselves from the most disadvantaged segments of the minority population. One response to those who see charter schools and vouchers as enabling segregation is suggested by the analysis we have offered in this book.

Whatever the virtues or failings of charters and vouchers might be, our analysis would indicate that their impact on school racial compositions is simply moot because the middle class of all racial and ethnic backgrounds have already managed to extricate themselves from schools where racial and socioeconomic isolation poses the greatest problems. However, some observers have offered evidence that school choice may actually help to desegregate schools through making choices more widely available, rather than relying on command and control.

The Civil Rights Project at UCLA (formerly the Harvard Project on School Desegregation and the Harvard Civil Rights Project) under the leadership of Gary Orfield has long been a proponent of judicially mandated deseg-

regation. In the introduction, we described Orfield and his associates as leading advocates of an aggressive return to command and control policies of
redistribution. Not surprisingly, the Civil Rights Project is highly critical of
school choice reforms.[43]

The organization has consistently argued that allowing families to make
their own school choices undermines the goal of redistributing students by
race. As we pointed out at the beginning of this book, the Civil Rights Project
has attributed continuing de facto segregation and any trends toward resegregation to a lack of political will to force redistribution, a position that we
have argued is untenable in the face of the evidence.

Unsurprisingly, the activists/scholars of the Civil Rights Project have
taken strong positions against vouchers and charter schools. In the book
*Educational Delusions? Why Choice Can Deepen Inequality and How to
Make Schools Fair*, Gary Orfield and fellow Civil Rights Project researcher
Erica Frankenberg argued in 2013 that charters and vouchers were part of a
second movement for choice, following the first one that impeded and opposed desegregation from the 1970s onward.

Orfield and Frankenberg argued that vouchers and charters were part of
an individualistic and anti-government ethos, akin to the attitudes that turned
educational policies away from massive efforts to achieve fairness by reduc-
ing individual decision-making in an earlier era.[44] Fairness, in this view,
requires taking choices away from individuals. Orfield and Frankenberg do
not deal with the problem of how to make individuals cease making decisions in the best interests of their own children.

Another critic of school choice, Christopher Bonastia, has argued that
"the hidden history of the charter school present lies with two responses to
school desegregation, both of which sought to weaken centralized bureau-
cratic control of public education. The first came from white, Southern segregationists fighting to maintain whites-only schools by publicly subsidizing
private schools. The second came from the black and Latino community-
control movement of the late 1960s and '70s, in which families who found
themselves in de facto segregated schools in spite of legal prohibitions
against segregation spoke up."[45]

Critics such as those at the Civil Rights Project and Christopher Bonastia,
then, agree with us that there are deep connections between the contemporary
school choice movement embodied in charters and vouchers and the desegregation struggle that has lasted over a half-century. However, these critics take
a much dimmer view of the nature of these connections, maintaining that the
choice strategies are, on the one hand, ways of avoiding desegregation by
uncooperative whites and, on the other, frustrated responses by minority
families to the failure of political will that supposedly produced resegregation.

The argument that school choice segregates students is not universally accepted. We have suggested in this book that the issue of desegregation is frequently moot because charters and vouchers tend to serve students in districts that cannot be meaningfully desegregated. Other researchers, though, have argued that school choice can actually increase racial diversity in schools. In 2012, a group of researchers at the University of Arkansas looked at how charters had affected the racial compositions in Little Rock.

In chapter 4, we saw that despite Little Rock's nearly mythic status as a desegregation success, it had become a majority black, majority low-income school district following decades of judicially mandated desegregation. According to the 2012 study, Little Rock charter schools were less likely to be hyper-segregated than traditional public schools. The researchers' analysis of student-level data indicated that this was because most transfers out of the traditional schools to charters involved minority students leaving minority-dominated schools or white students leaving white-dominated schools for special programs.

Thus, at least in this school district, there was some evidence that charter schools functioned as a mechanism for desegregation, not as means for avoiding it. [46] In this instance, charter schools combined elements of voluntary transfer programs and special program magnet programs. We note, though, that the study did not provide evidence that school choice could desegregate the school system. Instead, it offered data showing that school choice could simply reduce the hyper-segregation in selected schools.

Apart from the issue of whether charter schools can lessen segregation in schools, some supporters have argued that charters advanced the civil rights goals historically associated with desegregation because having access to these types of schools gave choices to minority families. Thus, for example, in a *Wall Street Journal* interview in October 2013, New York parent Regina Dowdell, responding to mayoral candidate Bill de Blasio's intent to tax and restrict the city's charters, argued that school choice, in the form of charter schools, was a civil right.

In language that echoed earlier arguments for desegregation, Ms. Dowdell maintained that New York schools were divided between those in wealthier neighborhoods, which provided good educational opportunities, and others "who don't live in neighborhoods where the schools are up to par." [47] The analysis we have offered in this book suggests that the observation that this division exists is accurate. However, it is not simply a matter of wealthier neighborhoods being given good schools, while lower-income neighborhoods are given schools that are below par. The neighborhoods produce the schools.

The *New York Post* published an editorial on this topic, in which the newspaper pointed out that "ninety-three percent of charter school children in this city are black or Latino" and opined that "there was a day when minority children faced politicians fighting to keep them out of good schools. It's no improvement to have politicians who would keep them trapped in lousy ones."[48] Again, though, although being able to choose other schools might improve education for some minority children, if they were to move en masse to other schools, it is difficult to avoid expecting that the quality of those other schools would decline.

In their May 2014 editorial on the Orfield position on school desegregation, Stephan and Abigail Thernstrom argued that school choice can improve minority school performance without seeking unrealistic racial redistribution. They state that "Studies by Roland Frye and many other social scientists reveal that black and Latino students actually learn more rapidly when they transfer into a good charter school (or private schools where vouchers are available), even if the school has a racial mix—i.e., not a majority of white students—that passionate advocates of racial balance find objectionable."[49]

The Thernstrom argument is interesting because it implicitly discards the quest for equality through racial redistribution in favor of seeking improvements in quality for minority students. Readers will note that although we have argued in this book that school compositions are a major determinant of educational value, we have not claimed that this is the only influence on student learning. If one focuses on the best possible educational outcomes for disadvantaged minority students, rather than on a dream of uniform equalization, then the studies cited by the Thernstroms raise important possibilities for minority schooling.

The desegregation-school choice debate took on judicial dimensions when policy makers faced the question of whether enabling the families of individual students to make their own school choices would come into conflict with the command and control orientation of federal consent decrees. In a television interview about the new statewide Louisiana voucher program in April 2012, one of the present book's authors maintained that implementation of the program in school districts still under court supervision for desegregation could violate federal law.[50] Those school districts are still legally controlled by federal judges.

In August 2013, the U.S. Justice Department sued the state of Louisiana, claiming that the school voucher program was making segregation worse in the state, in which thirty-four of the sixty-eight school districts remained under desegregation orders. Louisiana Governor Bobby Jindal responded, in the words of the *Times Picayune* newspaper, that "because most voucher students are black . . . the program, in fact, promotes civil rights by opening access to school options."[51]

Longtime desegregation expert Christine Rossell bolstered the state's case in a report filed in November 2013. According to Rossell, sixteen districts using vouchers saw segregation go down, three of them by large amounts. Rossell reported that only four districts using vouchers saw racial imbalances increase.[52] On the other side, Erica Frankenberg, Gary Orfield's associate and co-author, working under contract with the Department of Justice, prepared a report on Louisiana's voucher program in late 2013.

Frankenberg's report supported the argument that the Justice Department should carefully monitor the state's voucher program for the program's influence on the racial composition of schools. Frankenberg concluded primarily that the vouchers were not advancing the cause of desegregation. She argued that a small number of predominantly minority schools may have had slightly greater minority populations with vouchers than they would have had without vouchers.[53]

As an aside, we note that Professor Frankenberg did not show familiarity with our own 2002 book that clearly demonstrated that school districts throughout Louisiana had already resegregated long before vouchers, during and in response to the very governmental mandates she and Professor Orfield enthusiastically embrace.[54] Given the de facto segregation of Louisiana schools, with or without vouchers, we suggest that arguments over the impact of vouchers on school populations should be irrelevant. The real question should be if and to what extent such programs can improve minority education.

DESEGREGATION, SCHOOL CHOICE, AND EDUCATIONAL QUALITY

Despite some evidence that charter schools and vouchers might help to redistribute a limited proportion of students by race, the desegregation goal of putting minority students together with white students played a much smaller part in the school choice reform program than it had in the desegregation movement. This is arguably at least in part because the demographics of urban schools had made the goal of racial balancing difficult, if not impossible, in many districts around the country.

However, school choice advocates retained many of the axioms of desegregation: The educational opportunities of students depend on which schools they attend. Minority students are systematically denied opportunities because they are concentrated in lower-quality schools. Moving minority students out of these lower-quality schools can address unequal opportunities among racial and ethnic groups.

Like advocates of forcible student redistribution through desegregation, advocates of voluntary student redistribution through school choice have generally glossed over the question of the extent to which school quality is a matter of receiving access to good institutions or a matter of the students, families, and communities with differing social resources creating good or bad institutions. School choice has been presented as a matter of getting out of schools that do not provide educational value. It has largely missed the way that education operates as a market of exclusivity.

In the debate over school choice and in legal challenges such as the voucher case in Louisiana, it was evident that the era of desegregation had established the official framework for considerations of educational policy. Supporters and opponents of competitive alternatives to traditional public schools were compelled to argue whether these alternatives were making schools more or less racially identifiable. This question predominated even when the matter concerned only a few percentage points of "racial identifiability" in one direction or another.

Both sides in this debate have generally skirted questions suggested by the present book, such as, if vouchers really did bring large numbers of disadvantaged students into a private school, would not that private school go down in quality? If the backgrounds of students constitute the most important influence on what happens in the classroom, will not charter schools need to become segregated by socioeconomic status and race, at least at the level of the classroom, in order to retain the most advantaged students?

We do not count ourselves among the true believers in contemporary choice-based alternatives to traditional public schools or among the dedicated enemies of these approaches. The evidence on whether these alternatives improve schooling for students in general and for disadvantaged students in particular is mixed. It often comes from highly partisan sources with strong inclinations toward confirmation bias in their respective preferred directions.

The Stanford University based Center for Research on Education Outcomes (CREDO) is one of the few sources of independent, non-activist data on charter schools. A 2009 study by CREDO found that the results of charter schools were mixed. A second study by CREDO, published in 2013, found that charter schools were making substantial gains.[55] Dr. Margaret Raymond, the director of CREDO, observed of the 2013 study that "charter schools are benefiting low income, disadvantaged, and special education students."[56]

One of the authors of the present book, writing about the apparent success of charter schools among the disadvantaged minority students of New Orleans, has suggested that school choice options such as charters may be an effective option for districts with students who are clearly failing in traditional public schools. However, districts should be cautious about experimenting with students who are flourishing in traditional public school settings.[57] When charter schools or vouchers are introduced into school systems with many students who already have good choices, this raises the distinct possibility that subsidies to the disadvantaged will diminish those choices.

Ultimately, projects for school reform, through competitive educational markets or by other means, need to try to detach themselves from the heritage of mandatory desegregation. Reform projects should be evaluated on the basis of how they improve the relative educational performance of the students who participate in them, not how they serve blueprints for social trans-formation. Since different groups of students have different needs, any given educational strategy can serve the needs of some students, and not others.

School choice reforms do recognize that education is a marketplace. However, programs of subsidized choice often fail to recognize just what kind of marketplace it is. Families will make educational choices for their own children, and families with greater economic and social resources will have a wider range of choices, which they will make in the interests of their own children. School reform efforts of any sort can be successful only to the extent that they realistically evaluate varying benefits and respect varying interests.

CHAPTER SUMMARY

Charter schools and school vouchers, the two strategies of the market-orient-ed school choice movement, came out of the long effort to desegregate schools, and these strategies have been heavily influenced by this effort. Although vouchers were initially attempts by whites to avoid desegregating schools, contemporary school choice has been driven largely by the failure of desegregation to improve education for minority students, as well as by more general concerns over school quality.

The school districts that we looked at earlier in this book almost all turned to school choice strategies after decades of coercive desegregation proved futile. A number of these districts have become heavily invested in school choice programs. Louisiana is at the forefront of both types of choice pro-grams, and the city of New Orleans has become a national center for school choice. The Recovery School District, controlling most of the schools in the city, consisted entirely of charter schools.

Both charter schools and vouchers have aimed primarily at extending choice to minority and socioeconomically disadvantaged students. Despite this focus, questions of whether choice can promote equality of educational opportunity and of how choice affects school populations are hotly debated. Again, the concerns of desegregation have driven these debates. However, we suggest that the issue of whether charter schools or vouchers increase or decrease percentages of minority students in schools is irrelevant because most white students have already withdrawn from minority dominated schools, and cannot be expected to return regardless of educational policy.

Market-oriented reforms may help to improve the quality of education for the most disadvantaged students. However, such reforms will not remake our society or redistribute educational opportunity. Subsidizing choices by means such as vouchers may enable some minority students to move into better school environments. However, massive subsidies also run the risk of becoming another kind of redistribution, diminishing the quality of education for the more advantaged and creating new incentives to seek new ways to maintain their advantages.

The logic of a competitive market, moreover, entails winners and losers. As we saw in the case of New Orleans, the district that has attracted the greatest national attention for its school choice reforms, inequality among schools tends to increase when schools compete. Since schools compete for students in the educational marketplace, this means that the inequalities of schools involve sorting out students into achievement groups, with the most successful schools those that manage to attract the top students.

Conclusion

Historically, Americans have placed a high value on competitive inequality among individuals. While we vary in our political and economic orientations, few of us believe that every person should receive rewards of occupational prestige or income equal to every other person. Instead, most of us are committed to the idea that outcomes in life should be unequal, but that our rewards should depend on our own energies and talents. Inequality resulting from membership in ascribed categories, such as racial and ethnic groups, contradicts our national dedication to the competitive inequality that we refer to as equality of opportunity.

School desegregation arose as part of the Civil Rights Movement, a reaction to the contradiction between equality of individual opportunity and the categorical inequalities of race and ethnicity. If segregated schools were placing young people at advantaged and disadvantaged starting points because of past actions by governmental agencies, then it made sense for government to repair the damage. In theory, this could be done by redistributing students among public schools.

The case for school desegregation, then, was morally compelling. Much of the continuing support for federal oversight to promote desegregation derives from its moral power, and those who argue for a return to aggressive measures usually do so from the most admirable motives. Nevertheless, as we have tried to detail in these pages, campaigns for racial redistribution in schools have failed. They have not failed because of any lack of political will, but because they run counter to the nature of the educational marketplace and to competition among individuals at the heart of our socioeconomic system.

The most recent reform efforts in education, school choice approaches, do recognize that education is a marketplace in which individuals make decisions. These approaches may, in some situations, improve schooling. However, the market-oriented reforms also suffer from misleading assumptions inherited from the desegregation era. They tend to assume that if students are showing poor results in a school, it must be because the school or the teachers in it are not offering the right product. These students can get the right product by receiving the right subsidies that allow them to shop elsewhere. This overlooks the collective agency of students, who together create the value of their schools.

What, then, should be done? We acknowledge that it is much easier to point out problems than it is to come up with solutions. We also acknowledge that we do not have any ideal solutions. At best, we can recommend not making the same mistakes as in the past. If shipping students around by race has neither equalized education nor improved the overall quality of schooling, then clearly school districts and federal agencies should put that approach behind them.

We suggest that educators should concentrate on academics and on improving academic outcomes, without trying to redesign our society. Because students come to schools from unequal backgrounds and because these backgrounds play a large part in shaping educational results, it is unrealistic to demand the same levels of performance from students of differing backgrounds or to demand the same levels of performance from schools that serve different population groups. Those who disagree with us on this point should respond with logic and evidence, not with slogans or exclamations of indignation.

We would like to emphasize some important developments that have been largely overlooked in the fog of war that has characterized much of the cacophonous school reform debate to the present time. For one, there is an increasing recognition from all quarters that the educational sector does indeed operate as a marketplace. This recognition, we argue, is a step in the right direction. By beginning from a rational starting point, we are more likely to devise educational policy that is rational.

There is another very important point that has not been trumpeted enough as a positive consequence of American educational policy that increasingly promotes school choice over governmental control and coercion. Even the proponents of school choice alternatives, such as the right to attend any school in one's district (including charter schools), or even the right to attend any schools in any other districts, do not often reflect on how this approach aligns so well with the sacred American value of the equality of educational opportunity.

We argue that this value is a more enduring value, with greater historical significance for our country, then in chasing the unrealizable, utopian goal of equalizing all educational outcomes. By recognizing that education in the United States (and most everywhere else) is a market of exclusivity, yet allowing individuals the freedom to participate in this marketplace with a minimum amount of government interference (but with some help, as in strong anti-discrimination laws and the provision of charters and vouchers), a more just and realistic approach may be possible.

Notes

INTRODUCTION

1. Carl L. Bankston III and Stephen J. Caldas. *A Troubled Dream: The Promise and Failure of School Desegregation in Louisiana.* Nashville: Vanderbilt University Press, 2002.

2. Stephen J. Caldas and Carl L. Bankston III. *Forced to Fail: The Paradox of School Desegregation.* New York: Praeger, 2005 (cloth); New York: Rowman & Littlefield, 2007 (paper).

3. For our more detailed description of this history, see Carl L. Bankston III and Stephen J. Caldas, *Public Education—America's Civil Religion: A Social History.* New York: Teachers College Press, 2009.

4. *Brown v. Board of Education of Topeka,* 349 U.S. 294 (1955).

5. Office of the Assistant Attorney General, Civil Rights Division, *Civil Rights Division Activities and Programs* (Washington, D.C.: Civil Rights Division, 2002).

6. Although desegregation was originally concerned with African American students, by the early 1960s it was also extended to other minorities, most notably Latinos (see the section on Los Angeles in chapter 3).

7. *Green v. County School Board of New Kent County, Virginia.* 391 U.S. 430, 88 S.Ct. 1689 (1968).

8. See Gary Orfield and Chungmei Lee. "Historic Reversals, Accelerating Resegregation, and the Need for New Integration Strategies: A Report of the Civil Rights Project/*ProjectoDerechosCiviles* (The Civil Rights Project: UCLA, August 2007), accessed January, 22, 2014, http://civilrightsproject.ucla.edu/research/k-12-education/integration-and-diversity/historic-reversals-accelerating-resegregation-and-the-need-for-new-integration-strategies-1/orfield-historic-reversals-accelerating.pdf.

9. Stephan Thernstrom and Abigail Thernstrom, "*Brown* at 60: An American Success Story." *Wall Street Journal,* May 14, 2014, p. A13.

1. THE POLITICAL ECONOMY OF EDUCATION AND EQUALITY
OF EDUCATIONAL OPPORTUNITY

1. For the view that none of the arguments in favor of the public provision of education are persuasive, readers may want to look at John R. Lott, Jr., "Why is Education Publicly Provided: A Critical Survey," *The Cato Journal* 7, no. 2 (Fall, 1987): 475–501.
2. See the classic article by Milton Friedman, "The Role of Government in Education," in *Economics and the Public Interest*, ed. Robert Solow (New Brunswick: Rutgers University Press, 1955), 123–55.
3. Anthony Downs, An *Economic Theory of Democracy* (New York: Harper, 1957).
4. Among the best-known criticisms of this sort are Samuel Bowles, "Schooling and Inequality from Generation to Generation," *Journal of Political Economy* 80 (June 1972): S219–51; and Samuel Bowles and Herbert Gintis, *Schooling in Capitalist America: Educational Reform and the Contradictions of Economic Life* (New York: Basic Books, 1976).
5. Joel H. Spring, *The Sorting Machine Revisited: National Educational Policy Since 1945* (New York: Longman, 1989).
6. Charles M. Tiebout, "A Pure Theory of Local Expenditure," *Journal of Political Economy* 64 (October 1956): 416–24.
7. For a summary and critique of the intellectual development argument for education in a democratic society and of the inculcation of values arguments, see Lott, "Why Is Education Publicly Provided."
8. U.S. Department of Education, National Center for Education Statistics, Common Core of Data (CCD), "National Public Education Financial Survey," 1989–1990 through 2009–1910.
9. Jonathan Kozol, *Savage Inequalities: Children in American Schools* (New York: Harper Perennial, 1992).
10. Thorstein Veblen, *The Theory of the Leisure Class: An Economic Study of Institutions* (New York: Macmillan, 1902).
11. Dave Barry. Accessed *The Miami Herald*, http://www.miami.com/mld/miamiherald/living/columnists/dave_barry/.
12. Jenny Anderson and Rachel Ohm, "Bracing for $40,000 at New York City Private Schools," *New York Times*, January 27, 2012. Accessed March 15, 2014, www.nytimes.com.
13. Ibid.
14. Eric A. Hanushek, "The Economics of Schooling: Production and Efficiency in Public Schools," *Journal of Economic Literature* 24 (1986): 1141–77.
15. Gary Burtless, "Introduction and Summary," in *Does Money Matter? The Effect of School Resources on Student Achievement and Adult Success*, ed. Gary Burtless (Washington, DC: Brookings Institution Press, 1996) 1–42, 3.
16. Anonymous communication, April 1, 2004.
17. Cited in Kristen King, "Expert: BR Losing Its White students," *The Advocate*, July 13, 1999, A1.
18. *Missouri v. Jenkins*, 115 S. Ct. 2038 (1977/1978/1984/1987/1990/1995/1997).
19. Paul Ciotti, "Money and School Performance: Lessons from the Kansas City Desegregation Experiment," *Cato Policy Analysis No. 298* (Washington, DC: Cato Institute, 1998).
20. Ibid., 1.
21. Ibid.
22. *Missouri v. Jenkins* II 515 U.S. 70, 115 S.Ct. 2038 (1995).
23. Tracy Allen, "Judge Grants School District Unitary Status," *The Call*, August 15, 2003. Accessed October 9, 2003. http://www.kccall.com/news/2003/0815/Front_Page/027.html.
24. John Hildebrand, "Roosevelt High School Reopens after $66.9M Renovation," September, 9, 2013, *Long Island Newsday*, Accessed October 23, 1013. www.newsday.com.
25. Bruce Lambert. "State Moving to Take Over Roosevelt School District," *New York Times*, April 17, 2002. Accessed October 23, 1013, www.nytimes.com.
26. Ibid.

27. The New York State School Report Card Fiscal Accountability Supplement for Roosevelt Union Free School District. Accessed October 23, 2013.Accessed November 17, 2013. https://reportcards.nysed.gov/schools.php?district=800000049648&year=2012.

28. The New York State Accountability Report 2011–12. https://reportcards.nysed.gov/schools.php?district=800000049648&year=2010.

29. John Hildebrand. "NYS takeover of Roosevelt Schools failed, Some Say," *Long Island Newsday*, June, 29, 2013. Accessed December 4, 2013. www.newsday.com.

30. Louisiana Department of Education, "2013 School Report Cards," Accessed January 23, 2014. http://www.louisianabelieves.com/data/reportcards/2013/.

31. See, for example, Stephen J. Caldas and Carl L. Bankston III, "The Effect of School Population Socioeconomic Status on Student Academic Achievement," *Journal of Educational Research* 90 (1997): 269–77.

32. Anderson and Rachel. Ibid.

33. Geraint Johnes, *The Economics of Education* (New York: St. Martin's Press, 1993), 5.

34. Adam Smith, *The Wealth of Nations* (New York: Random House, 1776/1977). Smith argued that the whole country benefited when everyone was free to pursue his or her own best economic self-interests without government interference.

2. SCHOOLING AS A COMPETITIVE MARKET

1. Among the many works that have found this are James S. Coleman and Thomas Hoffer, *Public and Private High Schools: The Impact of Communities* (New York: Basic Books, 1987); James S. Coleman, Thomas Hoffer, and Sally Kilgore, *High School Achievement: Public, Catholic, and Private Schools Compared* (New York: Basic Books, 1982); Valerie Lee, Todd K. Chow-Hoy, and David T. Burkam, "Sector Differences in High School Course-Taking: A Private School or Catholic School Effect?" *Sociology of Education* 71 (1998): 314–35; William Sander and Anthony C. Krautmann, "Catholic Schools, Dropout Rates, and Educational Achievement," *Economic Inquiry* 33 (1995): 217–33; Kevin C. Duncan and Jonathan Sandy, "Explaining the Performance Gap Between Public and Private Schools," *Eastern Economic Journal* 33 (2007): 177–91.

2. Robert J. Franciosi, *The Rise and Fall of American Public Schools: The Political Economy of Public Education in the Twentieth Century* (New York: Praeger, 2004), 90.

3. Julian R. Betts and Robert W. Fairlie, "Explaining Racial and Immigrant Differences in Private School Attendance," *Journal of Urban Economics* 50: (2001): 26–51; Richard J. Buddin, Joseph J. Cordes, and Sheila Nataraj Kirby, "School Choice in California: Who Chooses Private Schools?" *Journal of Urban Economics* 44 (1998): 110–34; Bruce W. Hamilton and Molly K. MacCauley, "Determinants and Consequences of the Private-Public School Choice," *Journal of Urban Economics* 29 (1991): 282–94.

4. Our calculations from Steven Ruggles and Matthew Sobek, *Integrated Public Use Microdata Series, Version 3.0* (1 Percent Census Sample), Minneapolis: Historical Census Projects, University of Minnesota, 2003.

5. Our calculations for Steven Ruggles and Matthew Sobek, 2003.

6. Quoted in Franciosi, *Rise and Fall of American Public Schools*, 141.

7. David Brasington, "Which Measures of School Quality Does the Housing Market Value?" *Journal of Real Estate Research* 18 (1999): 395–413; Donald R. Haurin and David Brasington, "School Quality and Real Estate Prices: Inter- and Intrametropolitan Effects," *Journal of Housing Economics* 5 (1986): 351–68.

8. Quoted in Bankston and Caldas. *A Troubled Dream* , 70.

9. U.S. Department of Education, National Center for Education Statistics, Schools and Staffing Survey (SASS), "Public School Data File," 2011–2012.

10. U.S. Department of Education, National Center for Education Statistics, Schools and Staffing Survey, Public School Data File, 2003–2004.

11. Spyros Konstantopoulos, Manisha Modi, and Larry V. Hedges, "Who Are America's Gifted?" *American Journal of Education* 109 (2001): 344–82.

12. U.S. Department of Education, National Center for Education Statistics, 2009 High School Transcript Study (HSTS).

13. Franciosi, *Rise and Fall of American Public Schools*, 142.

14. Ibid.

15. Bankston and Caldas, *A Troubled Dream.*

16. Ibid.

17. Myron Lieberman and Charlene K. Haar, *Public Education as a Business: Real Costs and Accountability* (Lanham, Maryland: Scarecrow Press, 2003). 83.

18. Kyle Spencer. "Way Beyond Bake Sales: The $1 Million PTA," *New York Times*, June 1, 2012. Accessed April 1, 2014. www.nytimes.com.

19. Kyle Spencer.

20. Myron Leiberman and Charlene K. Harr. *Public Education as a Business*, 86.

21. Ibid.

22. Kyle Spenser.

23. See Carl L. Bankston III and Stephen J. Caldas, "White Enrollment in Non-Public Schools, Public School Racial Composition, and Student Performance" *The Sociological Quarterly* 41 (2000): 539–50.

3. COMMAND AND CONTROL FAILURES

1. Events in the Baton Rouge case are drawn primarily from one of our earlier books and articles, See Bankston and Caldas, *A Troubled Dream* and Stephen J. Caldas and Carl L. Bankston III, "Baton Rouge, Desegregation, and White Flight," *Research in the Schools* 8.2 (2001): 21–32.

2. Quoted in Bankston and Caldas, *A Troubled Dream*, 86.

3. In Louisiana, the parish (county) is in most cases identical with the school district.

4. Quoted in Bankston and Caldas, *A Troubled Dream*, 96.

5. See Ibid., 92.

6. Quoted in Ibid.

7. Louisiana Department of Education, *Annual Financial and Statistical Report*, 2002–2003 (Baton Rouge, LA: Louisiana Department of Education, 2004).

8. Louisiana Department of Education, *Annual Financial and Statistical Report*, 2009–2010 (Baton Rouge, LA: Louisiana Department of Education, 2011).

9. Louisiana Recovery School District. "Schools in the East Baton Rouge Parish," accessed October 26, 2013, http://www.rsdla.net/maps/#parish=East Baton Rouge.

10. Louisiana Department of Education, "2011–2012 School Report Cards, Capitol High School," accessed October 26, 2013, http://www.louisianabelieves.com/data/reportcards/2012/.

11. Recovery School District. "Crestworth Learning Academy, Profile," accessed October 26, 2013, http://www.rsdla.net/schools/pdf/crestworth-la.pdf.

12. Recovery School District. "Dalton Elementary, Profile," accessed October 26, 2013, http://www.rsdla.net/schools/pdf/dalton-es.pdf.

13. Zachary Community School District, "Accountability," accessed October 12, 2013, http://www.zacharyschools.org/?page_id=104.

14. Danielle Drellinger. "Schools Excel Before Tests Get Tougher," *Times-Picayune*, October 26, 2013, 1A.

15. Rebekah Allen. "New City Sought for School District," *The Advocate*, June 24, 2013, 1A.

16. Drellinger, "Schools Excel," 1A.

17. Allen, "New City Sought," 1A.

18. Diana Samuels, "Report Finds Incorporation of New City Could Hurt East Baton Rouge Finances," *Times-Picayune*, December 8, 2013, A13.

19. Diana Samuels. "In Unincorporated Baton Rouge, Residents Chart Path to New City," *Times-Picayune*, November 27, 2013, A1.

20. Paul Delaney, "Chicago to Attempt to Integrate Schools After Success in Other Cities," *New York Times*, September 4, 1977, A6.

21. Lesley Oeslner, "Court Backs Zoning That in Effect Bars Low Income Blacks," *New York Times*, January 12, 1977, A1.

22. "3 Chicago Youths Injured at an Anti-Busing Rally," *New York Times*, September 12, 1977, A18.

23. "500 Chicago Students Walk Out Over Busing," *New York Times*, September 14, 1977, A16.

24. Nathaniel Sheppard Jr., "Effort to Integrate Chicago Schools Has Had Little Effect, Study Finds," *New York Times*, March 6, 1979, A14.

25. "Chicago Board Rejects School Desegregation Under U.S. Conditions," *New York Times*, October 18, 1979, B24.

26. Casey Banas, "City Must Involve Most Schools in Integration Plan," *Chicago Tribune*, September 28, 1980, sec. 1, p. 2.

27. Casey Banas, "School Board Oks New Bias Plan," *Chicago Tribune*, April 30, 1981, sec. 1, p.1.

28. John McCarron and Stanely Ziemba, "Still Highly Segregated, Data Show," *Chicago Tribune*, April 7, 1981,sec. 1, p. 1.

29. "School Bill $87,732 for Bias Pact," *Chicago Tribune*, February 11, 1981, sec. 5, p.1.

30. Jean Latz Griffin, "Schools Sue US for Integration Aid," *Chicago Tribune*, June 2, 1983, sec. 1, p. 1.

31. John Schmeltzer and John McCarron, "City School Aid Vetoed," *Chicago Tribune*, August 14, 1983, sec. 1, p. 1+.

32. Casey Banas, "379 Schools Vie for U.S. Funds," *Chicago Tribune*, December 29, 1983, sec. 2, p. 1.

33. Mary Ann Zehr, "Close to Home," *Education Week* 23, no. 6 (10 March 2004): 30–34.

34. Chicago Catalyst, "Federal Judge Ends Chicago School Desegregation Decree," accessed October 21, 2013, http://www.catalyst-chicago.org/notebook/2009/09/24/federal-judge-ends-chicago-schools-desegregation-decree.

35. Rosalind Rossi, "Kids Beg for Better Schools—Students Say the Desegregation Decree Failed Them," *Chicago Sun-Times*, January 23, 2009, 14.

36. "Chicago Public Schools: Stats and Facts," website of the Chicago Public School System, accessed October 21, 2013, http://www.cps.edu/About/At-a-glance/Pages/Stats;and_facts.aspx.

37. Steve Bogira, "Trying to Make Separate Equal," *Chicago Reader*, June 2013, accessed October 22, 2013, http://www.chicagoreader.com/chicago/segregated-schools-desegregation-city-suburbs-history-solutions/Content?oid=9992386.

38. Associated Press, "Judge Ends Desegregation Order in Dallas schools," *CNN.com*, June 6, 2003, accessed December 12, 2004, http://www.cnn.com/2003/EDUCATION/06/06/dallas.schools.ap/ .

39. "Busing of 17,328 Ordered in Dallas," *New York Times*, April 11, 1976, 33.

40. Dallas Independent School District Adopted Budget, 2000–2001.

41. Dallas Independent School District Salary Report, January 11, 2001.

42. We're indebted to Josh Benton of the *Dallas News* for passing along to us information on the desegregation experience in the Dallas ISD.

43. Associated Press. "Judge Ends Desegregation."

44. Texas Education Agency, *Academic Excellence Indicator System, 2002–03 District Performance* (TEA: Austin, Texas, 2004).

45. Dallas Independent School District. 2012. *2013 Fact Sheet* (Dallas, Texas: DISD).

46. Vanessa Everett, "Campuses Journey Through Desegregation," *Beaumont Enterprise*, August 24, 2003, 1+.

47. Ibid, 4.

48. Ibid.

49. Christine Rappleye. "Unburdened—District Out from Under Far-Reaching Federal Suit After 37 Years," *The Beaumont Enterprise*, August, 30, 2007, A1.

50. Jim Mann, "18 Years En Route, LA Busing Arrives at the Highest Court," *Los Angeles Times*, March 31, 1982, 1–2.

51. Robert Lindsey, "Anger in California," *New York Times*, March 5, 1978, E4.

52. David G. Savage, "School Integration, Crowding: Solutions in Conflict?" *Los Angeles Times*, October 27. 1985, sec. 2, p. 1.

53. "14,000 Apply for 'Magnet' Schools," *Los Angeles Times*, March 28, 1982, 25.

54. Ibid.

55. William Trombley, "Major Problems Face Magnet Schools," *Los Angeles Times*, April 12, 1982, 2.

56. Lee Harris and Tendayi Kumbula, "Many Parents Giving Up on Black Public Schools," *Los Angeles Times*, September 1, 1982: 1+.

57. Pamela Moreland, "Armor Doesn't Miss a Beat in Battle Against Busing," *Los Angeles Times*, June 6. 1985, 3.

58. Pamela Moreland, "Board Raises Ratio of Minority Enrollments for 48 L.A. Schools," *Los Angeles Times*, May 19, 1987, 1.

59. Pamela Moreland, "Valley is 'Getting Shafted,' Weintraub Says of Magnet Proposal," *Los Angeles Times*, November 14, 1987, 3.

60. Pamela Moreland, "L.A. Schools' White Limits at 11 Schools is Reinforced," *Los Angeles Times*, June 7, 1988, 1.

61. Elaine Woo, "Judge Tells NAACP to Settle Lawsuit," *Los Angeles Times*, June 21, 1988, 1.

62. Sandy Banks, "Minority Gains Limited in L.A. Busing Program," *Los Angeles Times*, June 17, 1990, 1.

63. Los Angeles Unified School District, District and School Profiles, accessed October 25, 2013, http://search.lausd.k12.ca.us/cgi-bin/fccgi.exe?w3exec=PROFILE0.

64. Tom Wicker, "'Stifling' Pasadena's Integration," *New York Times*, April 29, 1973, 17.

65. Tom Wicker, "Integration in Pasadena," *New York Times*, April 27, 1973, 37.

66. Ibid.

67. William Trombley, "Public Schools in Pasadena Achieve Gains as Strife Ends," *Los Angeles Times*, June 9, 1986, sec. 1, p. 3.

68. Ibid.

69. Anica Butler, "Pasadena Superintendent Wants to Phase Out Busing," *Los Angeles Times*, January 20, 2002, B10.

70. Anica Butler, Pasadenans Debate Plan to End Busing," *Los Angeles Times*, February 8, 2002, B1.

71. Pasadena Unified School District at a Glance, accessed October 25, 2013, http://pasadenausd.org/modules/groups/homepagefiles/cms/917180/File/About%20Us/At%20a%20Glance%202013.pdf.

72. Pasadena Unified School District. Escuela Primaria Altadena, Informe Escolar Anual 2011–2012, accessed October 25, 2013, http://www.axiomadvisors.net/livesarc/SARCIndexPDFs/19648816021505_11-12_2.pdf.

73. Pasadena Unified School District. Washington Middle School. School Accountability Report Card, accessed October 25, 2013, http://www.axiomadvisors.net/livesarc/SARCIndexPDFs/19648816021752_11-12_1.pdf.

74. Pasadena Unified School District. John Muir High School. School Accountability Report Card. http://www.axiomadvisors.net/livesarc/SARCIndexPDFs/19648811936103_11-12_1.pdf.

75. John Herders, "Challenge to the North on School Segregation," *New York Times*, February 15, 1970. sec. 4, p. 2.

76. "Antibusing Law for State Voided by Federal Court," *New York Times*, October 2, 1970, 1.

77. Lesley Oelsner, "Queens School Plan Stirs Racial Controversy," *New York Times*, April 12, 1971, 48.

78. Martin Arnold, "Racial Outbreak at South Shore High School in Brooklyn is Traced to Earlier Tensions," *New York Times*, April 30, 1971, 40.

79. Mia and Mitchell Vickers, *New York Times*, October 17, 1970, Letter to Editor.

80. "Integration Plan Hailed at School," *New York Times*, May 18, 1974, 35.

81. Gene I. Maeroff, "City Schools Hint Suburbs are Needed in Integration," *New York Times*, February 27, 1974, 1.

82. Marcia Chambers, "School Integration Goals Elusive in Changing City," *New York Times*, April 23, 1979, B1.

83. "Abandoning Andrew Jackson High," *New York Times*, April 27, 1979, A30.

84. Marcia Chambers, "U.S. Tells Queens to Desegregate a School," *New York Times*, August, 30, 1979, B3.

85. Ibid.

86. Ari L. Goldman, "Macchiarola Orders Whites Shifted to Nearly All-Black Queens School," *New York Times*, June 19, 1980, B5.

87. Gene Maeroff, "Imbalance in the Schools and the Dilemmas of Integration," *New York Times*, December 27, 1980, 25.

88. Ibid.

89. Ari L. Goldman, "Queens Parents Defy Macchiarola on Pupil Transfer," *New York Times*, February 2, 1981, B3.

90. Serge Schmemann, "Rosedale School Dispute: The Parents Feel Abused," *New York Times*, February 6, 1981, B1+, quote on B3.

91. Edward A. Gargan, "Police Evict Protestors Occupying Queens School in Integration Case," *New York Times*, February 8, 1981, 1+.

92. Ibid., 30.

93. Howard Sertan, letter, *New York Times* February 18,1981: 30.

94. Serge Schmemann, "White View of Schools Clash," *New York Times*, February 17, 1981: B1+, quote on B1.

95. Gene L. Maeroff, "U.S. May Aid Queens Racial Plan," *New York Times*, September 11, 1981, B2.

96. Enrollment data available on-line at www.nycenet.edu/daa/SchoolReports.

97. N.R. Kleinfeld, "Why Don't We Have Any White Kids?" *New York Times*, May 11, 2012, MB1.

98. Fernanda Santos, "To Be Black at Stuyvesant High," *New York Times*, February 25, 2012, MB1.

99. Ibid.

100. Kyle Spencer, "For Asians, Schools are Vital Steppingstones," *New York Times*, October 26, 2012, A18.

101. NYC Department of Education. "2013 New York State Common Core Test Results: New York City Grades 3–8," August 2013, accessed October 28, 2013, http://schools.nyc.gov/NR/rdonlyres/C2708C2E-9C5F-451F-B4CF-2B5DBFF87D93/0/2013MathELAResultsSummary.pdf.

102. Mark Nichols and Kim L. Cooper, "Segregation Creeps Back In," *The Indianapolis Star*, May 26, 2004, accessed November 15, 2004, http://www.indystar.com.

103. Jon Jeter, "Integrated Magnet School Leaves Students Poles Apart," *Washington Post*, February 13, 1998, A1+. Quote from p. A1.

104. Nichols and Cooper, "Segregation Creeps Back In."

105. Data on the racial composition of Indiana schools is taken from the school data information on the website of the Indiana Department of Education, accessed November 23, 2004, www.ideanet.doe.state.in.us.

106. Indiana Department of Education, accessed November 23, 2004, www.ideanet.doe.state.in.us.

107. "Excerpts from Supreme Court Decision Barring Detroit-Suburban School Merger," *New York Times*, July 26, 1974, 17.

108. Warren Weaver Jr. "Dual Schools Still a Problem But Now It Is in the North," *New York Times*, April 21, 1974, B5.

109. "U.S. Submits Brief in Integration Case," *New York Times*, February 24, 1974, 35.

110. "Excerpts from Supreme Court Decision Barring Detroit-Suburban School Merger," *New York Times*, July 16, 1974, 17.

111. Agis Salpukas, "Joy Is Expressed in the Suburbs, Reactions in Detroit Divided," *New York Times*, July 26, 1974, 17.

112. Ibid.

113. United States Census Bureau, "2007–2011 American Community Survey 5-Year Estimates," accessed October 24, 2013, http://factfinder2.census.gov/faces/tableservices/jsf/pages/productview.xhtml?pid=ACS_11_5YR_DP05.

114. United States Census Bureau, "2007–2011 American Community Survey 5-Year Estimates," accessed October 24, 2013, http://factfinder2.census.gov/faces/tableservices/jsf/pages/productview.xhtml?pid=ACS_11_5YR_DP03.

115. U.S. Department of Education, *Digest of Education Statistics*, Table 95. (Washington, D.C.: Department of Education, 2011).

116. Michigan Department of Education, *Annual Education Report: Detroit City School District*. Posted online 8/30/2013, Accessed October 24, 2013, http://detroitk12.org/schools/reports/2012-2013_annual_education_report/82010.pdf.

117. Bankston and Caldas, *A Troubled Dream*.

118. Lisa Frazier, "P.G. Braces for Major Changes," *Washington Post*, June 24, 1996, B1.

119. Lisa Frazier, "P.G. Schools Struggle with Racial Plan," *Washington Post*, April 2, 1996, C1+. Quote of Ms. Teasdale taken from p. C1.

120. Ibid., C6.

121. Lisa Frazier, "Judge Blocks Move by P.G. School Board to Ease Magnet Racial Quotas," *Washington Post*, July 9, 1996, B1.

122. Peter Pae, "In P.G., A New School of Thought," *Washington Post*, July 28, 1996, B1+

123. Lisa Frazier, "Prince George's's School Plan Hurt by Tax Revolt," *Washington Post*, December 1, 1996, B1+.

124. Charles Babington and Lisa Frazier, "Proposal Would End Busing, Settle Suit in Prince George's," *Washington Post*, October 21, 1997, A1+.

125. Lisa Frazier, "Judge Ends Busing in Prince George's," *Washington Post*, September 2, 1998, A1+.

126. 2013 Maryland Report Card, accessed October 18, 2013, http://msp.msde.state.md.us/Demographics.aspx?K=16AAAA&WDATA=Local+School+System.

127. 2013 Maryland Report Card, accessed October 19, 2013, www.mdreportcard.org/msa. These percentages are all higher than those we cited in our earlier volume *Forced to Fail*, apparently because of changes in the test categories.

128. Ibid.

129. Boston's Children First v. Boston School Committee, 183 F. Supp. 2d 382.

130. Katharine Q. Seelye. Boston Schools Drop Last Remnant of Forced Busing. *The New York Times*, March 14, 2013. Accessed at: www.nytimes.com.

131. Jennifer B. Ayscue, Alyssa Greenberg, John Kucera, Genevieve Siegel-Hawley and Gary Orfield, *Losing Ground: School Segregation in Massachusetts* (Los Angeles: UCLA Civil Rights Project, 2013).

132. Rossell, "The Evolution of School Desegregation Plans"; Massachusetts Department of Elementary and Secondary Education Boston Enrollment Indicators, Accessed online at: http://www.bostonpublicschools.org/files/DOE%20Profile%20Boston.pdf.

133. *US News & World Report*, "Top High Schools: Boston Latin," http://www.usnews.com/education/best-high-schools/massachusetts/districts/boston-public-schools/boston-latin-school-9285/student-body Accessed 2 Nov. 2013. Boston Public Schools, "BPS Facts, no. 19," Published April 2013, accessed November 2, 2013, http://www.bostonpublicschools.org/files/bps_at_a_glance_13-0425_0.pdf.

134. Tip O'Neill and Gary Hymel, *All Politics Is Local* (Holbrook, MA: Adams Media Corporation, 1995).

135. "Louisville Busing Found to Alter Housing Pattern," *New York Times*, May 27, 1977, A9.

136. Steven V. Roberts, "Mixed Results of Integration Typified in Louisville School," *New York Times*, March 16, 1978, A23.

137. Ibid.

138. Iver Peterson, "Louisville, Once Violent, Then Calm, Is Now Edgy," *New York Times* November 18, 1979, D1.

139. United States District Court, Western District of Kentucky at Louisville, Civil Action no. 3:98-CV-262-H.

140. Kentucky Department of Education, *2010–2011 Kentucky Performance Report* (Frankfort, Kentucky, 2011).

141. *Parents Involved in Community Schools v. Seattle School District No. 1 et al*, 551 U.S. (2007).

4. MARKET OPTIONS AND ILLUSIONS OF SUCCESS

1. Rone Tempest, "Troubled Arkansas School Becomes Best in State," *Los Angeles Times*, February 28, 1982, 1.

2. Peter Baker, "40 Years Later, 9 Are Welcomed," *Washington Post*, September 26, 1997, A1+. Quotation taken from p. A9.

3. *USA Today*. "Little Rock Desegregation Plans Go Back to Court," *USA Today*, September 18, 2011, accessed December 12, 2013, http://usatoday30.usatoday.com/news/nation/story/2011-09-18/little-rock-desegregation/50455078/1.

4. Richard D. Kahlenberg. A Report to the Little Rock School District on Using Student Socioeconomic Status in the Inter-district Remedy for *Little Rock School District v. Pulaski County Special School District*. August 9, 2013.

5. On the "lavish praise" heaped on the Charlotte school system after desegregation, see Stephen Samuel Smith, *Boom for Whom? Education, Desegregation, and Development in Charlotte* (Albany: State University of New York Press, 2004).

6. Quoted in Ibid., 60.

7. Ibid., 62.

8. Ibid., 63.

9. Roslyn Arlin Mickelson, "White Privilege in a Desegregating School System: The Charlotte-Mecklenburg Schools Thirty Years After Swann," in *The End of Desegregation?* eds. Stephen J. Caldas and Carl L. Bankston III (New York: Nova Science Publications, 2003) 97–119.

10. Smith, *Boom for Whom?*, 83.

11. Quoted in Alison Moranta, "Desegregation at Risk," in *Dismantling Desegregation: The Quiet Reversal of Brown v. Board of Education*, eds. Gary Orfield, Susan E. Eaton, and the Harvard Project on School Desegregation (New York: New Press, 1996), 195.

12. Sue Anne Presley, "Charlotte Schools are Scrambling," *Washington Post*, November 8, 1999, A3.

13. Smith, *Boom for Whom?*, 6.

14. Ann Doss Helms, "Schools Ruling Led to a Decade of Change—End of Race-Based Assignment Launched Ripples Whose Merit is Still Debated, and Fresh Calls for Vision," *The Charlotte Observer*, September 10, 2009, B1.

15. Test results are taken from the Charlotte-Mecklenburg Schools website, accessed November 8, 2013, http://www.cms.k12.nc.us/departments/instrAccountability/schoolPerformance.asp.

16. Much of the account of the Wisconsin case is drawn from Jack Dougherty, *More Than One Struggle: The Evolution of Black School Reform in Milwaukee* (Chapel Hill, NC: University of North Carolina Press, 2004).

17. Ibid., 36–39.

18. Ibid., 149.

19. Paul Delaney, "Wisconsin Ponders a Plan for State to Legislate Desegregation of Four Schools in Milwaukee and Suburbs," *New York Times*, April 13, 1975, 22.

20. Dougherty, *More Than One Struggle*, 153.

21. Ibid.

22. Wisconsin Information System for Education, Data Dashboard, accessed October 24, 2013, http://wisedash.dpi.wi.gov/Dashboard/portalHome.jsp.

23. Milwaukee Public Schools. Suburban School Opportunities: Chapter 220 Program for Milwaukee Students for Fall 2013 (Milwaukee: Office of Family Services, February 2013), 1.

24. University of Wisconsin-Milwaukee Employment & Training Institute. *Socio-Economic Analysis of Issues Facing Milwaukee Public School Students and Their Families* (Milwaukee: Employment & Training Institute: 2013), 21.

25. MPS NAEP Data, Mathematics; MPS NAEP Data, Reading, the Milwaukee Public Schools website, accessed October 25, 2013, http://mpsportal.milwaukee.k12.wi.us/portal/server.pt/comm/assessment/415/assessment/38462.

26. Where not otherwise noted, much of our discussion of the St. Louis case is drawn from Amy Stuart Wells and Robert L. Crain, *Stepping Over the Color Line: African American Students in White Suburban Schools* (New Haven: Yale University Press, 1997). Wells and Crain provide an excellent case study of St. Louis, although their perspective and conclusions differ from ours. While we admire their work, we would take issue with their ad hominem characterizations of the white suburbanites who disagreed with inter-district busing as simply historically uninformed "resistors," contrasted with the "visionaries" who supported the program.

27. "Historical Background, Voluntary Interdistrict Choice Corporation, accessed October 17, 2013, http://www.choicecorp.org/HistBack.htm.

28. Hon. William Clay in the House of Representatives, July 16, 1999.

29. Joy Kiviat, "Could School Choice Save St. Louis?" *School Reform News*, December 1, 2000, accessed December 4, 2004, http://www.heartland.org/Article.cfm?artId=10832.

30. Missouri Assessment Program (MAP), 2010–2013. St. Louis City Disaggregate Data by Race/Ethnicity, accessed October 28, 2013, http://dese.mo.gov/schooldata/four/115115/mapd-none.html.

31. Wells and Crain, *Stepping Over the Color Line*, see the map on p. 254.

5. THE EDUCATIONAL MARKETPLACE AND THE RISE OF THE SCHOOL CHOICE MOVEMENT

1. No Child Left Behind Act of 2001, Pub. L. No. 107-110, 115 Stat. 1425 (2002).

2. William C. Knaak and Jean T. Knaak,"Charter Schools Education Reform or Failed Initiative?" *The Delta Kappa Gamma Bulletin* 79, no. 4 (2013): 45–53.

3. Knaak and Knaak. 465–47

4. U.S. Department of Education. "States Open to Charters Start Fast in 'Race to the Top,'" accessed January 11, 2014, http://www2.ed.gov/news/pressreleases/2009/06/06082009a.html.

5. Eli Ginzburg, "The Economics of the Voucher System," *Teachers College Record*, 72, no. 3 (1971): 3735–82.

6. See The Friedman Foundation for Educational Choice website at http://www.edchoice.org/ for more information.

7. Jackolyn Matthews, "The Milwaukee School Voucher Initiative: Impact on Black Students," *The Journal of Negro Education* 75 (2006): 5195–31.

8. James Forman, "The Rise and Fall of School Vouchers: A Story of Religion, Race, and School Politics," *UCLA Law Review* 54, no. 3 (2007): 6475–604. Quotation from p. 566.

9. Carl L. Bankston III and Stephen J. Caldas, *Public Education — America's Civil Religion: A Social History* (New York: Teachers College Press, 2009).

10. National Conference of State Legislatures, "School Vouchers," accessed January 13. 2014, http://www.ncsl.org/research/education/school-choice-vouchers.aspx .

11. District of Columbia, Public Schools. "Facts and Statistics," accessed January 13, 2014, http://dc.gov/DCPS/About+DCPS/Who+We+Are/Facts+and+Statistics.

12. Kimberly Dishongh and Cynthia Howell, "Math, Science School Gets Nod for Charter—Opening Goes to Planned LR Charter," *Arkansas Democrat-Gazette*, January 13, 2004, 1.

13. Lynn Bonner, "Legislature Votes to Lift Cap on Charter Schools," *The Charlotte Observer*, June 10, 2011, 10B.Vanessa Willis, "3 Charter Schools Now Open in Area," *The Charlotte Observer*, August 19, 2007. 9S.

14. Matthew Haag, "More Students Enroll in Charter Schools," *Dallas Morning News*, November 27, 2012, B1.

15. Paul G. Vallas, "Making the Grade: Chicago Schools CEO Tells How He Rescued a Failing System," *The Denver Post*, April 18, 1999,.H1.

16. "Build on Successes of Charter Schools," *Chicago Sun-Times*, December 3, 2012. 23.

17. Patrice Manuel, "School Choices Grow—Charter Schools Thrive, Local Officials Say," *The Beaumont Enterprise*, February 18, 2001, SS16.

18. Alan Bonsteel, "Too Many Schools Fail Their Students," *Daily News of Los Angeles*, March 28, 2006, N13.

19. "Charter School Movement Grows in LAUSD, California," *Daily News of Los Angeles*, November 7, 2013, 4.

20. Brian Charles, "Pasadena Rosebud Academy Defies Odds," *Pasadena Star-News*, September 23, 2011, 1.

21. Jennifer Chambers, "More Enroll in Charters than DPS," *The Detroit News*, December 11, 2013, A1.

22. Charles Upton Sahm. "Choice, Accountability, and Achievement," *City Journal*, 23 , no. 4 (2013), accessed January 10, 2014, http://www.city-journal.org/2014/eon0109cs.html.

23. Milwaukee Department of Public Instruction, "Milwaukee Parental Choice Program," accessed January 10, 2014, http://sms.dpi.wi.gov/sms_choice.

24. Erin Richards, "Leaders Discuss Split of MPS Schools / Meeting Examines Removing Low Performers," *Milwaukee Journal Sentinal*, August 25, 2013, 1.

25. Harold Bell, "Charter Schools are Making their Mark in Indianapolis," *Indianapolis Examiner*, April 28, 2010, 1.

26. "Indiana Voucher Use Nearly Tops Nation / Could Take Lead If Growth Continues," *Evansville Courier & Press*, October 14, 2013, 5A.

27. Jennifer Chambers, "More Enroll in Charters than DPS," *The Detroit News*, December 13, 2011, A1.

28. Prince George's County Public Schools, Office of Charters and Contract Schools, accessed January 7, 2014, http://www1.pgcps.org/charters/.

29. William F. Weld. "Charters on Edge of Ed Reform." *Worcester Telegram & Gazette*, June 28, 2013, A10.

30. Academy of the Pacific Rim website. http://www.pacrim.org/apps/pages/index.jsp?uREC_ID=89050&type=d&pREC_ID=168567&hideMenu=1. Accessed June 25, 2014.

31. KIPP Massachusetts website. http://www.kippma.org/kabms-about.php. Accessed June 25, 2014.

32. Neighborhood House Charter School website. http://www.thenhcs.org/our-school/fast-facts/ Accessed June 25, 2014.

33. Chuck Mason, "Kentucky Education Summit Focuses on Charter Schools," *The Daily News*, August 22, 2012, 1.

34. Elisa Crouch, "Nurturing Success Amid Setbacks," *St. Louis Post-Dispatch*, September 6, 2013, A1.

35. See Carl L. Bankston III and Stephen J. Caldas. *A Troubled Dream: The Promise and Failure of School Desegregation in Louisiana* (Nashville: Vanderbilt University Press, 2002)

36. Louisiana Department of Education. *Expanding Quality Options: Louisiana Type 2, 4, and 5 Charter Schools.2013–2014 Annual Report.* (Baton Rouge, LA: Louisiana Department of Education, September, 2013).

37. Bankston and Caldas, 2002; Carl L. Bankston III, "What Can New Orleans Teach Us?" *Contexts* 12, no, 3 (2013): 17–18; Carl L. Bankston III, "Race, Poverty, and Policy in the Wake of Disaster," *Sociological Forum* 28 (2013) 361–79.

38.   Danielle Dreilinger, "N.O. Tops List of Charter Enrollment—85% of Students Attend Such Schools," *Times-Picayune*, December 11, 2013, B01.

39.   Lyndsey Layton, "In New Orleans, Major School District Closes Traditional Public Schools for Good." *Washington Post*, May 28, 2014, http://www.washingtonpost.com/local/education/in-new-orleans-traditional-public-schools-close-for-good/2014/05/28/ae4f5724-e5de-11e3-8f90-73e071f3d637_story.html, accessed July 13, 2014.

40.   Carl L. Bankston III, "What New Orleans Can Teach Us." *Contexts* (Summer 2013).

41.   Ibid.

42.   Cowen Institute for Public Education Initiatives, *The State of Public Education in New Orleans: 2013 Report* (New Orleans: Tulane University, July, 2013).

43.   See the official position of the Civil Rights Project on school choice reforms on their website at: http://civilrightsproject.ucla.edu/research/k-12-education/integration-and-diversity/choice-without-equity-2009-report?searchterm=charter+schools.

44.   Gary Orfield and Erica Frankenberg.*Educational Delusions? Why Choice Can Deepen Inequality and How to Make Schools Fair* (Berkeley: University of California Press, 2013)

45.   Christopher Bonastia, "Charter Schools' Segregationist Roots," *Contexts* 12, no. 3 (2013): 25.

46.   National Center for the Study of Privatization in Education, Teachers College, Columbia University. "Choosing Charter Schools: How Does Parental Choice Affect Racial Integration?" October, 2012, accessed January 14, 2014, http://www.ncspe.org/publications_files/OP214.pdf.

47.   *Wall Street Journal* "Opinion: Why School Choice Is a Civil Right," Video interview conducted 10/11/2013, accessed October 12, 2013, http://live.wsj.com/video/opinion-why-school-choice-is-a-civil-right/8AB7BBCE-7D4B-45C5-8EE2-9F702CF6AF5D.html?mod=djemEditorialPage_h.

48.   Post Editorial Board. "Meet New York's Charter School Movement," Editorial published October 9, 2013, accessed October 13, 2013, http://nypost.com/2013/10/09/meet-new-yorks-charter-school-movement.

49.   Stephan Thernstrom and Abigail Thernstrom, "Brown at 60: An American Success Story." *Wall Street Journal*, May 14, 2014, p. A13.

50.   Louisiana Public Broadcasting. 2013 (April 26) "Louisiana, The State We're In," accessed January 13, 2014, https://www.youtube.com/watch?v=5JdpQli0NPk.

51.   Danielle Dreilinger Report Concludes Vouchers Improved Integration a Bit—New Ammo Found in Fight with Feds," *Times-Picayune*, November 14, 2013, A6.

52.   Dreilinger 2013 (November 14). P. A 06.

53.   U.S. Department of Justice. *United States Memorandum in Response to the State's Analysis Filed November 21, 2013*, accessed January 13, 2014, http://www.gov.state.la.us/assets/docs/Brumfield%20U%20S%20%20Mem%20%20re%20Expert%20Report%20Doc%20%20248.pdf; Danielle Dreilinger, "Louisiana School Voucher Data Show Need to Monitor Racial Balance, Federal Report Says," *Times-Picayune*, December 25, 2013, A1+.

54.   See Carl L. Bankston III and Stephen J. Caldas. *A Troubled Dream.* Readers should be cautioned to read all of the research on school desegregation and school choice skeptically, including and especially research emanating from partisan think tanks such as the Civil Rights Project of UCLA. Confirmation bias and echo chamber effects run deeply in the literature on these intensely political topics.

55.   Center for Research on Education Outcomes (CREDO). 2013. *National Charter School Study*, accessed January 15, 2014, https://credo.stanford.edu/documents/NCSS%202013%20Final%20Draft.pdf.

56.   Center for Research on Education Outcomes (CREDO). 2013. "Charter Schools Make Gains, According to 26-State Study," accessed January 15, 2014, http://credo.stanford.edu/documents/UNEMBARGOED%20National%20Charter%20Study%20Press%20Release.pdf .

57.   Bankston, "What New Orleans Can Teach Us."

Index

CPSIA information can be obtained at www.ICGtesting.com
Printed in the USA
BVOW02s1507200615

405214BV00003B/4/P